Just Stories

Just Stories

How the Law Embodies Racism and Bias

Thomas Ross

Beacon Press
Boston

Beacon Press
25 Beacon Street
Boston, Massachusetts 02108-2892

Beacon Press books
are published under the auspices of
the Unitarian Universalist Association of Congregations.

00 99 98 97 96   7 6 5 4 3 2 1

Text design by Sara Eisenman
Composition by Wilsted & Taylor

Library of Congress Cataloging-in-Publication Data can be
found on page 162.

I dedicate this book to my mother, Elizabeth O. Ross.

Law reflects but in no sense determines the moral worth of a society.
— Grant Gilmore, *The Ages of American Law*

Contents

Preface

My father grew up in the 1920s and 1930s in Pocomoke City, a small town on the Eastern Shore of Maryland. He told me stories of those days.

Pocomoke was, and is, a quiet town of modest white clapboard homes, churches, a "downtown" of small shops, a drugstore with a soda fountain, and a movie theater. Most of its residents have lived there for generations. The dark and tranquil Pocomoke River runs through the town. It seems a world away from the overdeveloped, bustling, and condominium-littered coast of Ocean City, Maryland, less than an hour to the east. It also seems apart from the trendy Eastern Shore communities where the young, rich professionals of D.C. flock for summer retreats. Pocomoke has always reminded me, instead, of the sleepy Southern towns of South Carolina and Georgia.

During my father's time, Pocomoke City had a sizable black population that lived in a parallel universe of rigid separation and economic oppression. Segregation was highly formalized and pervasive. Separate housing, separate schools, separate seating at the movie theater, separate bathrooms, separate water fountains, and so on. The town imposed a sundown curfew on blacks. When blacks and whites came together, as on a public street or in a work environment, strict codes of behavior applied: black people always had to acknowledge their subservience, by their posture, physical actions, and manner of speaking.

The economic subjugation of blacks was revealed in the circumstances of my father's household. My grandfather, so far as I can discern, did not possess significant income or wealth. He worked at various jobs, including a stint as mayor. Yet their life was comfortable and gracious — in large measure because, for pocket change, black women cleaned the house, made the meals, and did the laundry.

Thus my father grew up in a community that humiliated and subjugated its black citizens. Of course, the white citizens of Pocomoke would have been deeply offended by such a statement. To them, no humiliation or subjugation existed precisely because they believed blacks to be inferior and that cheap wages were just compensation for workers unfit for more complex occupations. Like the slave masters of the century before, the whites of Pocomoke presumably believed that they had "elevated" black people to an appropriate social and economic status.

My father left Pocomoke to attend college, and except for visits to his family he never went back. I never knew him to be other than someone who despised racism; he and my mother taught me as a child that racism was terribly wrong. On the other hand, my father never said or suggested that he felt guilty or responsible for the society of his childhood and its terrible treatment of his black neighbors. I don't think of my father as being responsible for the system of apartheid in his hometown. I am not even sure that he should have felt guilty about the comforts he enjoyed by virtue of that system of economic subjugation. I am sure, however, that his life was somehow forever tangled up with the legacy of Pocomoke.

The educational resources of the town were devoted to my father and the other white students and not to the young black men and women across the tracks. The sense of confidence he drew from his academic, athletic, and social successes arose from a system stacked in his favor because he was white. Even the clean and comfortable home in which he grew up was the product of a system that left blacks with no real bargaining power with respect to their own labor. My father could never give back what had been taken from others and given to him. While neither responsible nor simply guilty, he was complicit.

I had a different childhood. I grew up in a series of essentially all-white suburbs. No black women scrubbing the kitchen floors, no curfew, no racially divided movie theaters. Yet the de jure, and later de facto, segregation of my upbringing in America in the 1950s and 1960s worked to my advantage also, and to the disadvantage of my black contemporaries.

I attended public schools in New Jersey, Florida, and Virginia. Until high school I never shared a classroom with a black student, and even the high school I attended was almost entirely white. In the fall of 1967 I entered the University of Virginia. In response to litigation, the university was in the process of admitting its first black students. It would be several more years before it would admit women to the college, again, only after litigation.

I do not know firsthand the nature of the educational experience of my black contemporaries. While I sat in white classrooms, they attended "their own" public schools. Presumably, while I attended the University of Virginia, most blacks, except for the handful of brave young men who integrated the university, either skipped college or attended one of the black colleges in Virginia. I do know that throughout my years of education the state's resources were disproportionately directed to white schools. I also know that I grew up without having to deal with the negative presumptions that attached to my black contemporaries.

I do not see myself as responsible for the racially separated school systems that I inhabited, or for the racism that accounted for them. I do not think it is a matter of guilt for me. On the other hand, like my father, I am complicit. I can never give back the advantages I enjoyed by growing up in the 1950s and 1960s in a society that stacked the educational, social, and employment deck in my favor by virtue of my race.

And complicity doesn't stop with the inequalities of the past. As I cannot give back the advantages of my childhood or erase the disadvantages experienced by my black contemporaries, I also cannot avoid the continuing advantages I experience while living in a culture still gripped with prejudices that accord to me an assumption of worthiness that it denies to blacks, women, and others deemed different by the dominant class. This is the terrible and unwanted gift I receive every day of my life. And the fact that I receive it, wanted or not, keeps me in a state of complicity.

This circumstance is not unique to me. Whatever one's family history, we all live in a culture in which being a white as opposed to a member of a racial minority, being a man as opposed to a woman, being materially well off as opposed to poor, brings one into a state of complicity. Even those who reject stereotypes cannot escape the correlative advantages which our culture accords to them. We are all tangled up in it.

Yet we who are advantaged are not merely complicit. Most of us still harbor some version or degree of prejudice, and the body of contemporary law that most directly affects the lives of blacks, women, and poor people embodies and sanctions these prejudices.

I have explored the pathology of this law in writings over the past six or seven years. As a white man who has never lived in anything close to poverty, I can add nothing to the literature in the way of personal narratives of the experience of prejudice and intolerance; instead, I have explored the process of the construction of the law, and in particular the role of narrative in that construction. When I began this scholarly enterprise, my stated ambition was to advance the cause of reform by revealing clearly the presence of our worst prejudices in the law itself. I imagined that most of us would reject a body of law within which were embedded stories of racism, sexism, and class prejudice. Today I am less hopeful.

This book represents an overview of this scholarly journey. Chapter 2, "The Rhetorical Tapestry of Race," is based on two previously published essays: "The Rhetorical Tapestry of Race," published in the *William and Mary Law Review* in 1990, and "Innocence and Affirmative Action," from the 1990 *Vanderbilt Law Review*. The article "The Rhetoric of Poverty: Their Immorality, Our Helplessness," published in the *Georgetown Law Journal* in 1991, is the source for Chapter 3. Finally, Chapter 4 is based on the paper "Despair and Redemption in the Feminist Nomos," published in 1993 in the *Indiana Law Journal*.

I have addressed in turn the categories of race, poverty, and gender. This construction is convenient but potentially misleading. It is convenient because it permits a focused analysis of each of these important strands of law and cultural prejudice. It is misleading because it suggests that the law and the individual's experience of law and prejudice are similarly compartmentalized. This is not the case.

The law in actual operation is more complex than such compartmentalization might suggest. Taking the example of the current "case of the century," the state's law of murder as applied to O. J. Simpson surely incorporated the fact that the defendant was black. In other words, race mattered in the Simpson trial. But other things also mattered, most notably the defendant's wealth and celebrity status. These things allowed Simpson to assemble a "dream team" of defense lawyers and a cadre of high-priced expert witnesses. But his wealth and status had yet another effect. After all, a large measure of the shock value of the case came from the incredulous quality of it all: O. J. Simpson butchered his ex-wife and Ron Goldman? The initial incredulity, which as time passed evaporated in the minds of most white Americans, was largely a product of Simpson's celebrity status, but it was also a product of his wealth and general social position. Imagine instead that the defendant in the Nicole Brown / Ron Goldman slaying had been a poor black man without social status. Such a defendant would not only have had to make do with an overworked public defender as his lawyer, he would also have lacked something else that favored O. J. Simpson, the fact that a person of wealth and status seems in the dominant narratives of this culture to be less likely to be capable of brutality than a person without these attributes. Thus, Simpson was not merely a black defendant, he was a black, rich, famous, physically attractive defendant. All of this mattered.

In the aftermath of the Simpson verdict it seemed as though black America and white America had witnessed two different trials. Most white Americans not only saw the verdict as a terrible injustice, they were also at an utter loss to understand the opposite reaction by most black Americans.

The racial divide that "emerged" from the Simpson verdict was a product of narrative. By "narrative" I mean the stories that reflect our personal and collective experience, and thus embody our values and worldview. Most black Americans possess, as part of the narratives of their community, stories of police misconduct and brutality. For them, the idea that Simpson was framed by a massive police conspiracy is utterly plausible. Even those African Americans who doubted the existence of a conspiracy in this particular case viewed the verdict with the assumption that such police misconduct in their communities is a common reality. Possessing that assumption and those narratives, even an observer who harbored doubts about Simpson's innocence might justify the verdict as the "sending of a message" to police and to white America.

Most white Americans, in contrast, do not possess narratives of police as routinely lying and framing innocent defendants. They see such misconduct as extraordinary, aberrational. Thus they couldn't believe that a massive police conspiracy existed in the Simpson case. And they certainly couldn't comprehend any justification of the verdict grounded in the need to send a message — a message about what? Possessing their own narratives, all that most white Americans could see in the Simpson case was a guilty black man set free by a mostly black jury. How could anyone cheer such an outcome? they wondered.

Narratives and the prejudices they contain are complex and overlapping. Moreover, the issues I have chosen to focus upon here represent an incomplete list of the prejudices that inhabit our law. This book specifically examines the racism directed at African Americans, but Asian Americans, Latinos, Hispanic Americans, and Native Americans are also subject to racism. The pervasive and powerful homophobia that afflicts this country is also not analyzed here, but if I make my case for the law's embrace of these prejudices against blacks, women, and the poor, the implications are clear for the other terrible prejudices that grip our society.

Today many Americans express their exasperation at the persistent claims to victimization advanced on behalf of blacks, women, people in poverty, and other minorities. These self-proclaimed victims, it is said, need to stop whining and start working. A central character in this cultural dialogue is the "innocent" white man, seen as the true victim of contemporary times, assaulted by the effects of affirmative action and by a society that denies him the respect and regard he has earned.

I have no great expectations that this book will immediately shake the claimed sense of innocence held by so many Americans today or change the social and legal agenda they advance. The political forces that today proceed with the dismantling of affirmative action and the "end of welfare as we know it" seem nearly irresistible. When, as a child, I traveled the South in the 1950s and 1960s, I saw chain gangs of black men working alongside the road. It now appears that my grandchildren will be more likely to witness that specter again than they will be to see the world of racially integrated communities and schools that I once imagined for them.

PREFACE

Perhaps this book, like a small boat butting against the bow of a huge barge, is unlikely to alter the basic course of things. Still, it is a more useful and, to me, attractive endeavor than to merely tag along in the wake of the monstrous vessel that is our new conservative social agenda.

Acknowledgments

I began my law teaching career in 1979 at the Vermont Law School. Grant Gilmore, who spent most of his career at the Yale Law School, had joined the Vermont faculty a year earlier. For the first three years of my academic career — and what turned out to be the last three years of his — we were colleagues. The legal academy regarded Grant as one of its giants, and deservedly so. He was also a gracious, witty, and generous human being. Grant and his transcendently insightful writings have profoundly influenced my work.

I must also acknowledge the work of another legal scholar — a man I never met — Robert Cover, also of Yale. His stunning works of scholarship laid bare the nature of law and its inescapable connection to violence. He too was a giant.

I also owe a debt to the various contemporary scholars whose work generally falls under the labels of Critical Race Studies, Law and Narrative, Feminist Jurisprudence, and Law and Poverty. Their body of work represents an imaginative and important reconstruction of American law.

My friend Susan P. Koniak introduced me to the work of Robert Cover. In her own work, she has taken his insights to new places and enriched our scholarship. Her friendship and support for my work have been immeasurably important.

While writing the articles that formed the foundation for this book, I was blessed with extraordinarily able and committed research assistants: David Deep, Cheryl Dragel, Karen Eriksen, Michael Feigenbaum, Margaret Hackbarth, Maxine Krasnow, John Lockhart, Sonja Reid, and Julie Sadoff. I deeply appreciate their help and support.

At the University of Pittsburgh Law School Nadine Hamlett, my secretary, and the Word Processing Department, headed by LuAnn Driscoll, have provided consistent and professional support for my work.

Working with Beacon Press has been a pleasure. Executive Editor Deb Chasman encouraged me to take on this project and then patiently and graciously helped me keep it alive. Chris Kochansky edited the final draft with great skill and sensitivity.

Finally, and most importantly, I acknowledge the support of my family. My children — Katherine, Anthony, and Andrew — give me joy and hope. I honestly cannot find the words that would express adequately what Betsy's love and faith in me have meant in my life and my work.

Just Stories

1

Law and Narrative

All too many Americans believe that blacks are less intelligent and hardworking than whites, that women are less capable than men, and that poor people are lacking in character and moral integrity. Moreover, the state's law reflects, and in operation sanctions, these prejudices.

The simple explanation for this surprising feature of the law is that law will always accommodate the separation and subjugation of those whom the powerful fear and despise. These terrible prejudices inhabit our law not as aberrations or as breakdowns in an otherwise untainted process. They are basic building blocks in its construction.

Such a powerful indictment demands careful presentation and argument. The bulk of this book is devoted to a demonstration of the law's embodiment of racism, sexism, and the moral censure of the poor. To understand how and why the law embodies these prejudices, we must first understand what law is and how it comes to be. It is a much more complicated and interesting process than most suppose.

Many people suppose "the law" to consist simply and wholly of rules. We find these rules in legislatures' statutes, judges' opinions, and in less obvious but important sources like the regulations of a welfare agency or a police department's manual. For example, the Pennsylvania rape statute, until amended in 1995, read in part: "Rape — A person commits a felony of the first degree when he engages in sexual intercourse with another person not his spouse . . . by forcible compulsion."[1] Thus, when a man puts a knife to the neck of a woman and forces her to submit to sexual intercourse, he has committed the crime of rape, we would presume.

The simple "rules only" conception of law leads to a very simple mode of reform, namely, if you do not like the outcome of the law, just change the rules. Returning to the Pennsylvania rule above, if the knife-wielding assailant happened to be the woman's husband, he would not have committed the crime of rape. Unless you believe that the marriage vows include a woman's consent to being raped by her husband, and that such vows, if made, ought to be legally recognized, the Pennsylvania law seems outrageously wrong. Indeed, in the mid-1980s the Pennsylvania legislature changed the rule regarding a husband's criminal liability for raping his wife; under the new rule, husbands who used "forcible compulsion" against their wives to compel sexual intercourse could be convicted of "spousal sexual assault." Yet until 1995, a husband in Pennsylvania could not be charged with the rape of his wife, and spousal sexual assault was a felony of the *second* degree. In addition, the Pennsylvania spousal sexual assault statute incorporated a "fresh complaint" rule that barred any complaint not filed within ninety days of the assault.

The law of rape has been the subject of much contemporary reform. Legislatures have eliminated, or substantially modified, the spousal exception.[2] So-called rape shield laws preclude the admission of testimony about the victim's prior sexual history for the purpose of attacking the victim's virtue.[3] These changes have undoubtedly made a difference. Husbands are not utterly immune from criminal liability for rape, and defense lawyers can no longer parade a victim's sexual history in front of juries, at least not as easily as they used to do so.

Yet article after article describes the limited success of these reforms.[4] Women are raped every moment in this country, and the rapists, even when apprehended, often go unpunished. It is a disgrace that is repeatedly depicted in our public media. And no law reform effort seems to bring about real change.

If the law of rape were composed of nothing but the rules found in statute books and court opinions, we would expect to achieve complete and satisfying reform through the rewriting of those rules. But the whole of the law is composed of more than the rules, and to know what else constitutes law is to know why the reform of rape law by rewriting its rules is inherently an exercise in frustration.

Any woman who is raped (and any man who rapes) quickly learns the incomplete and misleading quality of the rules only conception of law. The law of rape is administered by the state's agents, beginning with the police officers at the scene. Police officers may facilitate, or make more difficult, the woman's complaint. In her illuminating work *Real Rape*, Susan Estrich begins with a story of her own experience. The police officers who responded took her complaint seriously once they determined that the assailant was a stranger and a black man — or, as the police officers described him, "a crow" (Estrich is white). When Estrich told them that the man had also stolen her wallet and car, they indicated that this was good because he had committed the crime of robbery, a crime that the system would take seriously.[5] The police encouraged, or at least did not discourage, her complaint. Yet in making their judgment they apparently thought that the race of the assailant, the absence of prior relations, and the presence of other criminal acts were each relevant to their response to the assault upon her, even though the formal legal rules make no mention of any of these considerations. Had Estrich been black, or her assailant a former lover, or her wallet and car left behind, the police might have discouraged, even refused, her complaint. If this had happened, how would one describe the law of rape as she experienced it? However described, the abstract text of the formal rules would fail to capture that experience.

Police officers are not the only state actors whose choices constitute the law of rape. Prosecutors may choose to press or not press the prosecution, or, most commonly, may make a plea bargain with a woman's attacker. If a case goes to trial, judges make choices that have an impact on the woman's experience of that trial. For example, the judge will determine the boundaries of the cross-examination of the woman by the defense counsel. That cross-examination can be utterly harrowing and humiliating, and it can have an important impact on the jury's decision. Juries declare guilt or innocence, thus making a choice on behalf of the state. The choices and actions of the state's agents — police, prosecutors, judges, and juries — determine the victim's and the defendant's experience of the law of rape. Some women, knowing the experience that awaits them, choose to keep silent. For these women, and for women who press their cases only to see them disappear in the discretionary choices of police or prosecutors, the formal rule criminalizing the act of rape may seem a hollow precept. They were raped and the state did nothing, they would say.

In the academic world, the rules only conception of law has all but disappeared. Although substantial disagreement about the nature of law continues, the academy understands, finally, what rape victims, criminal defendants, and any person who has entered this realm of law knew all along: that the law of the state is realized in the choices and actions of the state's agents, whether those agents are justices of the Supreme Court or bureaucrats at the local welfare office.[6]

This understanding can lead to a second mode of reform. What's wrong with the law of rape lies in the actions of some of the state's agents. Police officers who treat rape victims with disbelief, prosecutors who are reluctant to bring cases to trial, judges who preside over the courtroom humiliation of rape victims, and juries that acquit defendants on the flimsiest of grounds — or convict them on illegitimate grounds — are the problem. The problem is one of infidelity to law; these agents fail to enforce the law because of their personal prejudices.

In response to this sort of understanding we may tighten the rules to reduce the degree of discretion of those who act on behalf of the state. For example, mandatory sentencing rules limit the sentencing discretion of judges and juries. We may monitor more closely the behavior of the state's actors; we create, for example, citizen review boards to oversee the police. And the purge of state agents that fail to enforce the law in the way desired by the politically powerful is a time-honored method of law reform; thus, during the 1980s, the Republican administrations filled the ranks of the federal judiciary with judges who, in their view, would enforce the written law and not "make up" law to achieve some vision of social reform.[7] These methods of reform each, in one way or another, suggest that the problem is that the state's agents often fail to enforce the law.

But apart from rare instances of outright corruption, the state's agents, whether police officers, judges, juries, or whomever, see their behavior as consistent with law. They do not see themselves as lawless, or as subordinating law to mere personal prejudice. Returning to the example of the law of rape, several years ago the members of a Texas grand jury refused to indict an alleged rapist because the victim had asked him to wear a condom and had provided him with one. We must assume that the jurors concluded that a woman who provides a condom consents to intercourse, even when the man is a stranger who has broken into her home at night.[8]

[5]

The Texas grand jury members presumably did not see their behavior as lawless or even as a distortion of the law, but as a scrupulous application of the state's laws concerning rape.

A simple way to resolve this dissonance between the critic's sense of infidelity and the jurors' sense of fidelity to law is to conclude that the jurors have a mistaken conception of the law. But this answer presupposes that there is a single and determinate law and that sometimes the state's actors fail to comprehend it. Thus, when the Texas grand jury failed to indict, we could say that the jurors had simply miscomprehended the law of rape and applied a false conception of that law, one built from their personal and inapt prejudices. The jurors may have subjectively thought they were acting according to law but we know better.

In fact, in the Texas rape case, the prosecutor took the case before a second grand jury and finally got an indictment, and ultimately a conviction.[9] One might conclude that the Texas story reveals the existence of a true law, expressed in the second decision, contrasted with a mistake of law by the first grand jury. But what if there had been no publicity, no outcry other than the victim's? What if the Texas case had been treated as virtually all rape cases are treated, that is, without publicity and thus with enormous and virtually unchecked discretion lodged in the state's agents? The first decision would have stood as the state's expression of the law; the rapist would have gone free.

When the state's agents apply their understanding of law and bring to bear the specter and reality of force and violence that is the state's, this is the *state's law*. This is true even when the agent's choices are later changed by another agent's actions. Returning to the Texas case, while you could say that the first grand jury miscomprehended the law of rape, the jury's refusal to indict was a choice backed by the state's power for as long as it existed as the state's choice, and what could we call this choice backed by power but the state's law?

The problem is not that the state's agents sometimes miscomprehend the law; they comprehend it all too well. They determine the state's law; their acts *are* the state's law. To anyone who supposes that this is merely a semantic game, a linguistic skirmish over the definition of the term "state's law," I suggest that they imagine looking into the barrel of a police officer's revolver or staring up at a judge who has the power to send you to the living hell we call prison. Although another police officer may arrive on the scene and countermand the one pointing a gun at you, or another judge may reverse the order sending you to prison, this will not happen often. Even when it does, for a time the state's law is precisely what that police officer or judge says it is. And if you doubt and resist, the officer or the marshals under the judge's command will impress this jurisprudential point upon you in no uncertain terms.

Yet sheer force is not law. It is not just the possession of power that makes the choices of the state's agents the state's law. For the actions of the state's agents to be "law" in any sense of the word, there must also be some coherent interpretation of a precept by which their actions can be understood. The 1991 beating of Rodney King by Los Angeles police officers and the riots that followed the initial acquittal of the officers provide a double context for this point. The police officers who rained blow after blow to the body of Rodney King undoubtedly brought the force and violence of the state to bear. They also presumably had some explanation in their own minds for their behavior. Yet it is hard to imagine any coherent interpretation of a legal precept that would transform that beating into an act of law. Thus, if we are prepared to say that their actions, to our mind, can only be seen as the product of a desire to hurt someone who made them angry or as the desire to teach a black man a lesson, we can brand this a lawless act. When we conclude that the state's agents have brought force alone to bear, we can say that there is no act of law. Thus, the *state's law* is a product of both power and meaning. It is in fact the practice of wielding force without law that defines totalitarianism.

The power component of the state's law is realized in the deployment of or in the refusal to deploy force. For example, in the violent aftermath of the first verdict in the trial of the police officers who beat Rodney King, the police withdrew from South Central Los Angeles and the nation watched South Central burn. This choice not to deploy force shaped the state's laws forbidding assault, arson, and other acts of violence; during the riot, the law that reigned in South Central was not the same as the law that reigned in the cozy suburb of Pacific Palisades. Of course, this dissonance in law is hardly restricted to times of riot. Typically, the state deploys all force necessary to assure substantial compliance with its criminal laws in the neighborhoods of the rich, while virtually turning over control of the streets of the inner city to the criminals. In saying this, I do not misunderstand the danger or difficulties of law enforcement. Rather, the point here is that our choices about the deployment of the state's force determine the state's law. There is not one simple law of murder in Los Angeles. To say "It is unlawful to commit murder" is to make a pronouncement of law that would be heard as serious and accurate in Pacific Palisades and, alternatively, as cruelly ironic if uttered in South Central.

To understand what the state's law is and how it comes to be, we must explore concepts which, like most fundamental ideas, are at once simple to express and hard to grasp. Expressed simply, the state's law is a product of the mix of rules and narrative, which together yield meaning, coupled with the state's commitment to that meaning. This basic yet elusive understanding of law was advanced by Robert Cover, a brilliant legal scholar, in his article "Nomos and Narrative," published in 1983.[10] In one way or another, most thoughtful members of the legal community possess some version of this understanding. Yet rarely have we thought through its implications.[11]

Even in the simplest situation, we discern the command and scope of a legal rule only by resort to narrative. Recall the simple precept of the Pennsylvania statute on rape — to engage in sexual intercourse by forcible compulsion is unlawful and is called rape. Imagine a stranger coming up to a woman in a dark parking lot, putting a gun to her head, and having sexual intercourse with her in the back seat of her car. This is surely rape. Imagine alternatively that the man is a former lover, the weapon is his hands, and the locale is her apartment. Is this rape? Deciding whether any but the simplest situation is or is not an instance of the crime of rape demands an act of interpretation that answers the question, What shall be the meaning of "forcible compulsion" in this particular instance of alleged rape? Whether answered by a judge, juror, prosecutor, or police officer, the act of answering that question is the same: the state's agent must fill the words "forcible compulsion" with meaning. That meaning can only come through narrative.

"Narrative" as used here is a name for both the vividly told or remembered stories we ordinarily think of as narrative, and the less clear imaginings we bring to bear. The meaning of "forcible compulsion" will flow from such narratives. If a juror possesses stories about women as desirous of "rough" intercourse, as physically capable of resisting assault in the absence of a weapon other than the man's body, as notoriously untrustworthy in matters of sex — in other words, if the juror brings to bear any of some of the most commonly held narratives about women, sex, and rape — then "forcible compulsion" means guns and knives and strangers coming out of the darkness of the parking lot and does not mean the insistent demands, the pushing and shoving, of a former lover in the woman's apartment.

The meaning of "forcible compulsion" never comes from abstractions or verbal reformulations alone. For example, to say that forcible compulsion is the compulsion that would overpower the resistance of any reasonable woman gets us nowhere. What is that "compulsion" and who is the "reasonable woman"? Moreover, to utter an abstraction like "forcible compulsion should be interpreted to assure that a woman's choices about sex are as respected as a man's choices about to whom to give his wallet" also gets us nowhere. The juror who brings the stereotypical stories about women to bear will have little difficulty squaring his or her judgment with such an abstraction. In the world of such a juror, women who have sex are as protected as men who part with their wallets: in each instance the act is criminal if accomplished by "force" and not criminal if accomplished by words. (This juror would be unlikely to note that in fact the criminal law punishes the taking of a man's money by fraud but generally not the taking of a woman's right to choose whether or not to have sex by fraud.)

Wherever there is law, there is narrative. Cover wrote, "No set of legal institutions or prescriptions exists apart from the narratives that locate it and give it meaning."[12] The case *Brown v. Board of Education* was built on the precept of the Fourteenth Amendment to the U.S. Constitution, which commands every state to accord to each citizen the "equal protection" of the laws; segregated public schools violated this precept, said the *Brown* Court. Yet in the late nineteenth century, in *Plessy v. Ferguson*, the Supreme Court had concluded that the state laws that constituted our system of racial apartheid were consistent with the equal protection precept of the Constitution.[13]

The justices of the *Plessy* Court and those of the *Brown* Court brought different sets of stories to the precept of equal protection. The *Plessy* justices brought stories of the inherent inferiority of the black race, of the dangers of civil unrest posed by racial integration, and of the self-imposed quality of any stigma that black persons might feel by virtue of the legal system of apartheid. They found that the apartheid laws upheld in *Plessy* treated blacks and whites equally; just as blacks were forbidden to occupy the railroad cars set aside for whites, whites were banned from the railroad cars set aside for blacks. Moreover, apartheid protected blacks and whites from the violence thought likely to erupt if the two races commingled. Thus, in the imagination of the *Plessy* justices, racial apartheid did not deny blacks the equal protection of the laws.

The *Brown* justices, in contrast, brought different stories to bear. The focal point of their opinion is the image of the black school-children sitting in segregated schools, their "hearts and minds affected in ways unlikely ever to be undone." The segregation laws stigmatized these children, in the stories of the *Brown* justices. These laws, on the other hand, did not stigmatize the white children. Thus the laws did not yield equal protection.

The evolution in law from *Plessy* to *Brown* is a larger story than this simple depiction. Still, the basic premise is accurate. From *Plessy* to *Brown*, the constitutional precept remained the same. The meaning of that precept, however, always depended on the narratives brought to bear. Different narratives yielded different meanings.

Precept and narrative together yield the meaning that is expressed as a norm, as a rule for behavior. The norms that bound our conduct are often not derived from the state. We discern these norms from various sources. We sit in church pews, synagogues, mosques and are taught the meanings of our religious precepts as revealed by the privileged narratives of our faith. For example, the precept of the Golden Rule is explicated by the story of the Good Samaritan. Within our families, we pronounce rules of conduct that are a product of the precepts and narratives we possess. The rules of behavior we as parents impose for the dinner table, long car trips, and other settings derive in large measure from the stories we have about our own childhood. All of these activities involve the combination of precepts and narratives to generate a meaning that is a rule for behavior. But without the third element, without some commitment, we cannot generate law. If I am unwilling to see the meaning realized in action, I am not engaged in the activity of generating law. For example, if I as a parent am unwilling to stand behind my pronounced rules regarding long car trips, my stated norm ceases to merit the name "law," and our car trips become bedlam.

On the other hand, when individuals and communities make meaning and have a commitment to that meaning, they make law. If, for example, a religious community is willing to demand that the meaning that evolves from their sacred texts is to guide the conduct of each and every person that would claim membership within that community, and if they demonstrate this commitment both by their own conduct and by the exclusion of those who disobey their laws, they then have made law. In fact, much of our constitutional law has arisen out of the clash between the state and religious groups like the Jehovah's Witnesses. Similarly, our commands to our children become the law of the family when we are committed to those norms. The often chaotic experience of family life is a ceaseless reminder of the distinction between the generation of law as something to which we are committed and the generation of meanings to which we are unwilling to commit.

The idea that religious communities and families may generate their own law is not some idiosyncratic appropriation of the meaning of the term. If law is understood as the norms that govern our conduct, the vast bulk of those norms for most persons is generated not by the formal processes of the state but instead by the institutions of family, community, and religious faith. Moreover, those laws not generated by the state often conflict with the formal laws of the state and call us to choose between competing laws. Most people facing that choice cede to the state for the simple reason that the state possesses the apparatus of force and violence that commands obedience. But often people do not subordinate their law to the state's law and the result is either the public act of civil disobedience or the more common act of breaking the state's law and hoping to get away with it. Thus we may cheat on our taxes, violate the posted speed limit, cut across someone else's private property, or otherwise break the state's law. Even when we give ground to the state's law, it does not mean that we no longer possess the law that we subordinate at that moment. We might, for example, choose to obey the state's law but to protest that law in various public and private ways that pose risks for us of state and perhaps private retaliation. The so-called pro-life demonstrators usually do not break into clinics or kidnap pregnant patients. The actual deployment or the threat of state force makes them stop short of such intervention. Yet they still run risks for their law and thereby demonstrate a commitment, albeit one that stops short of martyrdom.

When we look to our history, we see many prominent examples of groups of individuals and communities generating their own law and holding that law against the law of the state. These examples range from the inspirational acts of civil disobedience of the civil rights marchers of the 1960s to the shameful disobedience of the white racists who defied the commands of *Brown* and engaged in "massive resistance" to school desegregation. Each of these examples also shows the power of commitment. In time, the law of the civil rights marchers became the basis for formal precepts of the state's law, as exemplified by the various civil rights statutes passed by Congress in the 1960s, yet the law of the segregationists, while it disappeared as formal precept, is reflected even today in the reality of our children's lives.

Putting all these pieces of law together — precept, narrative, and commitment — we can return to the threshold question, What is the state's law and how is it generated? The creation of the state's law begins with the meaning that emerges when the state's agents bring their narratives to bear upon the formal rules of the state's law. When the police officers on the scene (most commonly male) bring their narratives of women and sex to bear upon the formal laws of rape, they generate a meaning that suggests whether a particular incident is or is not rape. That meaning becomes the state's law when the third element of commitment is supplied. Police officers demonstrate their commitment to that meaning when they use their authority and power to encourage, or discourage, the woman's complaint. If they choose to discourage the complaint, and if their authority is sufficient, they then determine the law of rape, at least for this woman and the man whom she accuses of violating her body. The officer's choice becomes the state's law.

Because the police, prosecutors, judges, jurors, welfare bureaucrats, and other persons who wield the state's power possess narratives within which blacks, women, and those in poverty are deemed different and less worthy, the state's law embodies those narratives. This is most obviously the case for the bluntly racist police officer or the arrogantly sexist judge. And although not every agent of the state is an overt racist, many are, and many more carry their narratives of prejudice only at the unconscious level.

We can make these claims about the state's agents simply because we know the pool from which they are drawn. The sad truth is that most Americans still possess, at least at the unconscious level, some version of these narratives. I certainly do. When I take my son to our HMO clinic and an unfamiliar black doctor walks in the room, I experience a sense of concern that I know is different from the feeling I would have if this new doctor were white. When I listen to a black man give a lecture and am struck by his eloquence, I know I am impressed in part because I expected less from him because he is black. I am ashamed of these feelings and assumptions and seek to slough them off as soon as I consciously discern them, yet I cannot altogether escape the racism I was taught for so long by my peers, my teachers, my television shows, and my segregated childhood (although not, thank God, by my parents).

The state's agents include people who, like me, still possess unconscious assumptions about blacks, women, and the poor. So long as those assumptions are discerned and dealt with, the choices of the police officer, the judge, and others will not fully embody the terrible stories we have been taught. But what happens when we do not catch ourselves, when our choices are influenced by those stories? When *we* are agents of the state, the law then embodies our stories. Moreover, the state's agents also include people who embrace prejudice at the conscious level. The police officers who responded to Susan Estrich's rape used racial epithets and judged the case to be "real rape" when they learned that the victim was white and the attacker black; obviously they had no interest in sloughing off their racism.

The bulk of this book is devoted to the demonstration of the pervasive presence of racism, sexism, and class prejudice in our law. In some ways, it will be a disturbing and depressing depiction, because law reform cannot be simply a matter of changing the rules. Changing the rules will make a difference — rules are part of the material out of which law is constructed, and the state's agents generally do take seriously the formal rules of law — but the agents' narratives are beyond the control of any legislature. The legislature can make a new rule and subject husbands to criminal liability for raping their wives, but no legislature can make a juror put aside the narrative of the entitlement of husbands to sex on demand with their wives; such a juror might accept the rule that a husband can rape his wife, yet see no rape when it is the wife's word against the husband's, or when the evidence of force is "merely" some bruises and scrapes.

We can reform the law of race, gender, and poverty. In fact, we have already reformed this law, if by reform we mean the partial, halting, sometimes regressive evolution we see looking back across our history. Our law no longer enslaves nor formally subjugates blacks as it did in the nineteenth century, and states can no longer command racially segregated schools, yet our white children and our black children still sit in segregated classrooms. And the law protects the preferences that account for such segregation by virtually forbidding the use of busing in order to break down the de facto segregation of America's public schools. Our work forces still exhibit a racial stratification, with blacks notably absent from many of the more lucrative and prestigious positions, and the law protects that stratification by, again, virtually forbidding the one remedy that might bring change — the use of affirmative action measures that demand a certain presence of blacks within the workplace.

Similarly, our law no longer denies women the right to hold and control property, the right to vote, the right to be a lawyer, as it did in the nineteenth century, yet in the latter half of the twentieth century this country refused to amend its Constitution to express the simple declaration that women were entitled to equality under the law.

Finally, our judges no longer speak of the poor as a "moral pestilence," as they did in the nineteenth century. Still, our construction of the law by which we provide assistance to those in poverty draws its coherence from our own version of the long-standing myth that poverty connotes moral weakness, if not degeneracy. The law sends poor people on nightmare journeys through Kafkaesque welfare bureaucracies. The law props up a system that offers poor children public schools that are so dreadful that anyone with the financial means to do so flees from them. We make it all tolerable, if not perfectly coherent, by telling ourselves that the poor are unwilling to work and otherwise undeserving. We tell ourselves that their poverty is the sad but just consequence of their weakness, and thereby tell ourselves that our wealth is a product of our strength.

If we seek to rid our law altogether of the narratives of racism, sexism, and class prejudice, we seek more than reform, we seek law's true redemption. We seek a law that reflects our true and complete embrace of equality.

Nothing in our history or experience would lead us to suppose that we will anytime soon rid ourselves altogether of our racism, sexism, and class prejudice, but the message of this book is that we ought to seek just such a redemption. We ought to seek it even though it is surely beyond our reach.

Redemption, of course, is always beyond us, whether it is redemption of our law, our society, or our individual selves. Grant Gilmore concluded his remarkable book *The Ages of American Law* with the following passage:

> Law reflects but in no sense determines the moral worth of a society. The values of a reasonably just society will reflect themselves in a reasonably just law. The better the society, the less law there will be. In Heaven there will be no law, and the lion will lie down with the lamb. The values of an unjust society will reflect themselves in an unjust law. The worse the society, the more law there will be. In Hell there will be nothing but law, and due process will be meticulously observed.[14]

Short of heaven, our law will always reflect our imperfect moral worth. We will always possess stories about "the others," those we fear and despise, whoever they may be. And the law will always embody those stories.

Nonetheless, we ought to embrace and pursue a redemptive vision of law. To understand why we ought to do so, we need to understand the last piece of what is "law." The narratives we bring to the formal rules of law are not just haphazardly chosen, they are inevitably connected with a vision of the world to come. Moreover, this world to come is always one we imagine to be just and righteous. Thurgood Marshall had a vision of a world in which our children would sit in racially integrated classrooms, and imagining this world to come gave coherence to the law he advocated. Even the white segregationists did not make their law out of stories about a world of black subjugation and the special advantages this subjugation created for the whites; instead, they too envisioned a world of perfect harmony, although their vision included a perfect separation which they imagined as just and righteous.

The simple truth is that law cannot be coherently constructed without a redemptive vision. The question for us is, Which vision shall we pursue? I say that we ought to pursue a vision of a world in which the law is wholly cleansed of the taints of racism, sexism, and class prejudice. We ought to do so not because we expect to create such a world, but because such a vision will shape the narratives that we bring to law and thus shape the law itself. And in doing so we will achieve for ourselves and our law the approximation of redemption that is our noblest possibility this side of heaven.

2

The Rhetorical Tapestry of Race

Nineteenth-century Americans lived in a truly racist society. Racist talk and racial epithets flowed through public discourse. Black persons were first enslaved, and later segregated and subjugated, by law. And the Supreme Court sanctioned all this in the name of the Constitution. In matters of race, it was a shameful and tragic period for the Court and the culture.

We live in a different time. Expressions of racial inferiority and other racist talk are no longer accepted forms of public discourse. De jure segregation is gone. And our Supreme Court, however controversial some of its choices on race may be, seems to be proceeding in a responsible manner. Whatever our shortcomings and disappointments on the matters of race, few of us suppose that we are creating a history for which those who follow will feel a sense of tragedy and shame comparable to that which we feel toward the Court and culture of the previous century.

I want to shake this comfortable sense of assurance about our historical standing and encourage us to rethink our assumptions about race. I hope to bring about a certain discomfort, and a rethinking of our choices, by showing that the essential rhetorical themes of the nineteenth-century laws we now discredit persist in the themes of our contemporary law. When we see that we talk and argue about race in much the same way as did our predecessors whose choices stain our legal history, we shall have good reason to reexamine the choices of our own time.

The Awful Magic of Rhetoric

Rhetoric — the art of persuasion and the chains of argument it produces — is a magical thing. It transforms things into their opposites. Difficult choices become obvious, change becomes continuity. Real human suffering vanishes as we conjure up righteousness. Rhetoric becomes the smooth veneer over the cracked surface of real and hard choices.

The excellent lawyer is always a master rhetorician. In a moment, this lawyer can construct multiple arguments for any given position, respond to assaults, make devastating attacks on the rhetoric of others. Such a lawyer seems to have an almost instinctive feel for spotting the suppressed and problematic premise in an argument, like a predator sensing the weak animal in a herd of prey.

This rhetorical facility is no happenstance. It is a product of our country's legal culture and history. The legal culture has elevated the art of rhetoric to a central position, and the judges who have an unambiguous claim to being the legal profession's heroes are those seen as excellent in both choice and rhetoric.

Robert Ferguson ascribed to Oliver Wendell Holmes, Jr., and to all judges who would be great, the dual cultural role of warrior and magician.[1] The judge as warrior makes the hard choice with regard to a question of law, the act of the warrior; with the choice made, he turns to us and makes it intellectually coherent and thus tolerable by his rhetoric, the act of the magician. This metaphorical description of the essence of great judging reveals the centrality of rhetoric.

The greatest challenge for the judge as rhetorician is to make coherent the choices that might divide us as a community. The greatest of these challenges throughout our legal history have been those triggered by race. From the judicial enforcement of the nineteenth-century fugitive slave laws through the most recent affirmative action cases, judges have tried desperately to explain the law's response to racial oppression. The stakes have often been frighteningly high. The apparent paradoxes have made the rhetorical work daunting. In the infamous nineteenth-century *Dred Scott* case, Justice Taney's awful magic somehow made the choice to deny black persons the status of citizens within a society ostensibly devoted to the principle of individual human freedom seem intellectually — as opposed to morally — coherent.[2] Again and again in our legal history, judges have spun this rhetorical magic around the issue of race, obscuring the conflicts and paradoxes, smoothing over choices for which we would later feel nothing but shame.

These special challenges have produced a special rhetoric, the legal rhetoric of race. This rhetoric exhibits much variety. Each judge, each case, each choice produced a unique magic. Yet a pattern emerges: the theme of white innocence runs like a thread through the rhetorical tapestry of race.

"White innocence" is the idea of the innocence or absence of responsibility of the contemporary white person. Nineteenth-century rhetoricians, both within and outside the legal community, advanced the idea in various ways. The defenders of slavery who grounded their arguments in the denial of the humanness of the slave, in the reduction of that slave to a chattel, were insisting on the innocence of the white slaveholder. Slavery was not, for them, a matter of subjugation and denial of the principle of freedom; it was instead a natural, even moral, disposition of another species of creature. In this vision of slavery, the white person is no more tainted by slavery than he would be by the penning and use of his cattle.[3]

A version of this view was expressed on the floor of the United States Senate in 1858 by Senator Hammond of South Carolina:

> In all social systems there must be a class to do the menial duties, to perform the drudgery of life. That is a class requiring but a low order of intellect, and but little skill. Its requisites are vigor, docility, fidelity. Such a class you must have. . . . It constitutes the very mudsill of society. . . . Fortunately for the South we have found a race adapted to that purpose to her hand. . . . Our slaves are black, of another, inferior race. The status in which we have placed them is an elevation. They are elevated from the condition in which God first created them by being made our slaves.[4]

Having "elevated" the black race, the white slaveholder had no reason to feel remorse.

For those whose racism was less virulent, the rhetoric embodying white innocence had to be constructed differently. In 1832, Professor Thomas Dew of William and Mary College published what historian George Fredrickson has called the "most thorough and comprehensive justification of the institution [of slavery]" of its time. In his essay, Professor Dew provided the perfect symbolic expression of the innocence of the white slaveholder as a man saddled with an inescapable burden:

> If ever a nation stood justified before Heaven, in regard to an evil, which had become interwoven with her social system, is not that country ours? Are not our hands unpolluted with the original sin? . . . Where is the stain that rests upon our escutcheon? There is none! . . . Virginia has nothing to reproach herself with — "the still small voice of conscience" can never disturb her quiet. She truly stands upon this subject like the Chevalier Bayard — *"sans peur et sans reproche."*[5]

The Chevalier Bayard was a French knight of the late fifteenth and early sixteenth century who lived a life of near mythical courage and purity. Bayard was thus the perfect symbol for the Southern white who wished to see slavery as an unfortunate burden thrust upon him by his ancestors, those who bore "the original sin."

The claim to innocence was often facilitated by the rhetorical depiction of the black person in the abstract, outside of any real and rich social context. Although abstraction is a rhetorical tool not unique to the rhetoric of race, it proved especially useful in race cases and pervaded the discourse on race in the nineteenth century. For example, in the infamous late nineteenth-century case *Plessy v. Ferguson*, establishing the constitutionality of the apartheid laws, the Court asserted that these laws did not necessarily connote the racial inferiority of the black race; after all, the law treated each race equally in that the exclusion of whites from railroad cars designated for blacks was as firmly and clearly expressed as the exclusion of blacks from white cars. This assertion makes sense only in the abstract context created in the opinion. Only by ignoring the real social context of the late nineteenth century could the Court say with a straight face, as they did in *Plessy*, that any racial stigma flowing from apartheid laws must be simply self-imposed.

Nineteenth-century legal argument obscured the degradation of blacks and absolved contemporary whites of responsibility for any images of degradation that might have shown through the filters of rhetoric. Thus the nineteenth-century judges made their choices intellectually coherent and smoothed over the conflict between the reality of subjugation and the abstract constitutional principles of freedom and equality.

Today we discredit *Plessy* and the other nineteenth-century cases on race. Yet the rhetorical themes of the last century are still essential themes in our contemporary rhetoric of race, both within and outside the domain of law. The contemporary battles are over school busing and affirmative action, not fugitive slave laws and apartheid laws, but those who reject the remedies of busing and affirmative action also insist on the innocence of the contemporary white person and often use the device of abstraction to do so. Although the precise rhetorical structures are different, the central theme of white innocence and the use of abstraction to obscure reality run through the tapestry of our legal and social rhetoric of race, then and now.

Rhetoric and Racism in the Nineteenth Century

The rhetoric supporting the institution of slavery was simply constructed in the sense that once one got past establishing the nonhuman nature of blacks, the rest was easy. If white people had any moral obligation in the matter, it was an obligation to use blacks to further the interests of a society from which black people were excluded. The horrific conditions of slave existence might even be seen as tokens of charity and benevolence to the black "brute." This particular line of rhetoric took various forms but always avoided any real conflict in values and principles by placing black people outside the community of humans.[6]

The arguments of the nineteenth-century justices seem not to partake of this virulent form of racism. Yet their rhetoric often worked in much the same manner, not explicitly denying but obscuring the humanness of black people by the use of abstractions, syllogisms, and legal vernacular. The principles of individual freedom and human equality — ideas that were at the core of Revolutionary and Constitutional discourse — ostensibly conflicted with the reality of slavery, and later in the century with the reality of the de jure segregation and oppression of blacks. Those judges who denied themselves the rhetorical move of the most virulent form of racism, the move of explicitly placing blacks outside the human community, had to be more sophisticated in their arguments.

The most skillful of these rhetoricians constructed exquisitely horrific rhetorical structures to justify choices that society has since discredited. The three examples I have chosen for analysis are the majority opinions in *Dred Scott*, *The Civil Rights Cases*, and *Plessy*.[7] These cases, we now say, form a tragic chapter in the Court's jurisprudence of race. Woven through the majority opinions in these cases, the theme of white innocence made intellectually coherent the subjugation of blacks.

Dred Scott *and Taney's Narrative of Subjugation*

Chief Justice Taney's opinion in the 1856 *Dred Scott* case stained the Court's history, virtually ruined the historical standing of its author, enflamed the passions of the abolitionists, and hastened the bloodbath of our Civil War.[8] Taney's opinion declared that Congress lacked the power to prohibit slavery in the Territories, thus striking down the laws that had regulated the extension of slavery, the Missouri Compromise. He also asserted that blacks, whether free or enslaved, were not citizens of the United States. To establish the latter assertion, Taney constructed the artifice of white innocence in an interesting way. He told the story of the subjugation of blacks through colonial times and into the Constitutional period. Taney cast blacks as articles of merchandise, possessing no rights that any white man was bound to respect. He also concluded that the meaning of the term "citizen" in the Constitution had to be interpreted according to the intentions and understandings of those who had drafted and ratified the Constitution in the late eighteenth century. Linking narrative and this interpretive theory, Taney built his intellectual edifice:

> The question before us is, whether . . . [blacks] compose a portion of this people, and are constituent members of this sovereignty? We think they are not, and that they are not included, and were not intended to be included, under the word "citizens" in the Constitution. . . . On the contrary, they were at that time considered as a sub-

ordinate and inferior class of beings, who had been subjugated by the dominant race, and, whether emancipated or not, yet remained subject to their authority, and had no rights or privileges but such as those who held the power the Government might choose to grant them.

It is not the province of the court to decide upon the justice or injustice, the policy or impolicy, of these laws. The decision of that question belonged to . . . those who formed the sovereignty and framed the Constitution. The duty of the court is, to interpret the instrument they have framed, with the best lights we can obtain on the subject, and to administer it as we find it, according to its true intent and meaning when it was adopted.[9]

Thus blacks were not citizens. This conclusion in turn denied blacks, free and enslaved, the ability to invoke the jurisdiction and power of the federal courts to protect their interests.

Taney's narrative reflected its ideological purposes. He chose to place his narrative in a particular place and time, and then from within that place and time he chose what pieces of that story to tell. Taney did not, for example, place any portion of his narrative in Africa, where the black person was part of a real and rich culture. He chose not to tell the story of seventeenth-century colonial life with its relative tolerance for black people.[10] Moreover, he finds virtually no place for the story of free blacks living in the Constitutional period.

Taney's carefully crafted narrative, coupled with his interpretive theory, established his own and his generation's innocence. Blacks simply were not citizens, not because Taney chose to deny them that status but because the Constitution could be read no other way.

The use of original intent as an interpretive theory is not unique to the *Dred Scott* case. Yet it helped Taney to push away responsibility for his choice. Depending on the extent of Taney's own racism, he may have felt little need to evade personal responsibility; nonetheless, his originalism theory permitted him to pretend that he was not saying blacks ought not be deemed citizens, but merely that the Constitution, properly interpreted, did not include them — and that the justice or injustice of this conclusion was not the Court's business.

In a more general sense, Taney's narrative suggested a naturalness to the subjugation of black people. Blacks, in Taney's story, were everywhere and always subjugated. This implied that their subjugation was a product of their natural difference rather than the brute force of white masters. This suggestion of naturalness or inevitability in turn mitigated the potential conflict between the reality of subjugation and the principles of freedom and equality.

The Civil Rights Cases *and the "Special Favorites" Argument*

In the years following the Civil War, the Reconstruction Amendments to the Constitution abolished slavery and formally guaranteed the rights of citizenship to blacks, and thus, in effect, negated the principles of *Dred Scott*. The scope and meaning of these amendments has been, from their beginning, a controversial issue.[11] In *The Civil Rights Cases*, decided in 1883, the Court held that the Reconstruction Amendments did not grant to Congress the authority to create the Civil Rights Act of 1875, Congress's effort to provide some source of statutory protection for Southern blacks in the waning days of Reconstruction.[12] Justice Bradley, writing for the majority, concluded that the amendments did not grant to Congress the power to enact a law that prohibited racial discrimination in public accommodations and conveyances. Bradley's opinion relied on the principle that the Constitution granted Congress only the power to regulate "state action." The proposed statute, he argued, regulated private action and not state action.

Justice Bradley's opinion contained one of the most outrageous examples of the use of abstraction in nineteenth-century rhetoric about race:

When a man has emerged from slavery, and by the aid of beneficent legislation has shaken off the inseparable concomitants of that state, there must be some stage in the progress of his elevation when he takes the rank of a mere citizen, and ceases to be the special favorite of the laws, and when his rights as a citizen, or a man, are to be protected in the ordinary modes by which other men's rights are protected. [13]

Bradley's assertion was fantastic. True, the statute sought to create a protection especially for black citizens, but this was in direct response to the reality of pervasive and brutal oppression of blacks by whites. The purpose of the federal statute struck down in the case was to create the possibility of some continued federal presence and power in the South to protect blacks as Reconstruction came to a close and the federal government began what ultimately became an abandonment of Southern blacks. The whites, of course, were not favored in the statute precisely because they were the oppressors.

Justice Harlan, in dissent, responded to the "special favorites" argument:

It is, I submit, scarcely just to say that the colored race has been the special favorite of the laws. What the nation, through Congress, has sought to accomplish in reference to that race is, what had already been done in every state in the Union for the white race, to secure and protect rights belonging to them as freemen and citizens; nothing more. The one underlying purpose of congressional legislation has been to enable the black race to take the rank of mere citizens. [14]

Harlan's opinion, unlike Bradley's, reflected some sense of the reality of nineteenth-century America, some sense of the actual social context in which the statute would have operated.

Bradley's opinion was similarly fantastical in its assertion that blacks were victimized only by the random acts of individuals and that victimized blacks could simply seek redress in the state courts:

The wrongful act of an individual, unsupported by any [state] authority, is simply a private wrong, or a crime of that individual; an invasion of the rights of the injured party, it is true, whether they affect his person, his property, or his reputation; but if not sanctioned in some way by the state, or not done under state authority, his rights remain in full force, and may presumably be vindicated by resort to the laws of the state for redress. [15]

Bradley's suggestion was disconnected from the reality of the social context. The wrongs for which redress might be sought were rapidly becoming official policy in the Southern states. [16] Redress in the state courts was a fanciful illusion.

By keeping his rhetoric above the field of play and in the strata of the abstract, Bradley was able to make assertions that were laughable in their real and operating context, and to smooth over the dissonance in the Court's exercise of its power to void a statute designed to address the real and pervasive oppression of black citizens. In Bradley's rhetorical world, the Civil War and the Reconstruction Amendments ended all forms of state-sanctioned racial oppression; all that was left were the random acts of individual lawbreakers, and the state courts, he claimed, would of course effectively redress those wrongs and punish the recalcitrant whites.

Bradley's opinion also stressed the potential for the victimization of the innocent white race. He conjured the specter of some future municipal code that would govern the private lives and choices of whites, compelling them to accept black persons into their communities on terms of equality. The federal statute, he wrote, "steps into the domain of local jurisprudence and lays down rules for the conduct of individuals in society towards each other, and imposes sanctions for the enforcement of those rules." [17] Thus the intrusion into the white man's prerogatives was for the majority the true violation of rights at stake in the case. By maintaining that white people were merely expressing preferences, and ignoring the context of a pervasively embraced ideology of racism, the Court guaranteed to whites their right to express and live out this racism.

Bradley's opinion at once obscured the degradation of blacks in the aftermath of Reconstruction and implied the innocence of the whites who were in fact responsible for this degradation. In Bradley's rhetorical world, blacks must assume "the rank of mere citizen" and not seek special favor or unearned advantage, and innocent whites must be protected against victimization by laws granting blacks such special favor.

Plessy *and the Self-Imposed Stigma*

In 1896, in the case of *Plessy v. Ferguson*, the Supreme Court reviewed a Louisiana statute that segregated railroad passengers by race, a statute that exemplified the proliferating new "Black Codes" that established apartheid throughout the South in the late nineteenth-century.[18] Justice Brown spoke for the majority of the Court and held the statute constitutional as a "reasonable" form of regulation. Brown found the statute's reasonableness in its connection with "established usages, customs, and traditions of the people, and with a view to the promotion of their comfort, and the preservation of the public peace and good order."[19]

The only problem with the "reasonableness" of the law was that it was grounded in a sanctioning of racism. The "traditions" were those of racism; the "comfort" was that experienced by whites who were legally protected from the physical proximity of blacks; and the threat to public peace was the specter of whites reacting violently to the efforts of blacks to take a place of social equality. Both the law itself and the reasons for the law that Brown advanced were expressions of the pervasive and especially virulent racism that gripped this country in the latter part of the century.

Nonetheless, the legal rhetoric of Brown's opinion in *Plessy* attempted to make the choice somehow intellectually coherent. Brown built his opinion on the assertion that segregation by law does not degrade or stigmatize the black person. "Laws permitting, and even requiring [racial segregation], in places where they are liable to be brought into contact, do not necessarily imply the inferiority of either race to the other."[20] Moreover, Brown asserted that any sense of stigma felt by a black person would be self-imposed. "We consider the underlying fallacy of plaintiff's argument to consist in the assumption that the enforced separation of the two races stamps the colored race with a badge of inferiority. If this be so, it is not by reason of anything found in the act, but solely because the colored race chooses to put that construction upon it."[21] After all, Brown argued, the segregation laws treat each race the same; whites are forbidden from sitting in the railroad cars set aside for blacks just as blacks are forbidden from sitting in those for whites. The laws do not express the inferiority of the black race; the laws treat each race equally.

These assertions seem patent nonsense to us now. And they were just as patently nonsensical in Brown's time and place. The purpose and effects of racial segregation laws throughout our legal history have been always the same — to express the ideology of white supremacy. These laws were a product of — and an expression of — racism, then and later. When a black person subject to laws commanding racial segregation in railroad cars felt thereby a sense of stigma, he or she had not misunderstood the message or revealed some idiosyncratic sensitivity, that person had heard and received precisely the message intended by those responsible for the law.

Only in some abstract conception of the society could one say with a straight face that these segregation laws were not premised on racism and did not express a message of racial inferiority. Only in this abstract conception could the argument that these laws represented "equal treatment of each race under the law" have any real power. Any real attempt to imagine the motivation for the passage of such laws or the effect these laws would have on black citizens unravels Brown's argument.

At several points in the opinion, Brown did leave the field of rhetorical abstraction and demonstrated the reality of racism. Specifically, Brown argued that if a state legislature dominated by blacks were to pass a racial segregation law like the one challenged in *Plessy*, the white race would not assume it was an expression of their inferiority. Here Brown stepped out of the realm of abstraction and unwittingly made a sensible comment on the society in which he lived, by implying that the very thought of a white man thinking himself inferior to a black man on account of race was lunatic. [22]

Brown revealed again his sense of the real society within which these laws operated in his concluding passage. He referred to the inherent problem in the implementation of a racial segregation law, that is, the problem of defining "white." Brown noted that this was typically done through a statutorily specified "blood" ratio. The state statutes on this subject differed. In some states "the predominance of white blood must only be in the proportion of three-fourths"; in other states "any visible admixture of black blood stamp[ed] the person as belonging to the colored race."[23] These laws defining the condition of being "white" were patently racist. The conception of "tainted black blood" is obvious when the slightest admixture can deny one the status of a white person.

Brown's opinion also embodied the theme of white innocence. The self-imposed stigma argument permitted whites to evade responsibility for any degradation felt by black people. Moreover, the racism expressed explicitly and implicitly throughout the opinion gave a naturalness and logic to de jure segregation, which, in turn, let the white person off the hook: blacks were different and inferior, thus to segregate blacks was a natural thing to do and not an act of oppression.

By considering the circumstances of the black person in an abstract context and by asserting the natural inferiority of the black race, Bradley's opinion rhetorically mitigated any possible conflict between the declared constitutionality of de jure segregation and the ostensible constitutional principle of equality. Thus, in *Plessy* — as in *Dred Scott* and *The Civil Rights Cases* — the Court relied on rhetoric embodying white innocence to deny or disguise the tragic reality of the enslavement and degradation of African Americans.

The Promise of *Brown*

In the United States of the twentieth century prior to *Brown v. Board of Education*, our tragic reality was apartheid. Post-*Brown*, the situation is different but nonetheless tragic. Black people constitute a disproportionate percentage of the poor. Segregation has shifted from de jure to de facto. School busing to remedy segregation is now a historical artifact. Affirmative action is everywhere under assault. And contemporary versions of "welfare reform" are likely to lock in the racially disproportionate face of American poverty.

In a society committed to racial equality, in a society where racism is no longer part of the official ideology nor part of accepted political and legal discourse, how are we to account for the separation and economic deprivation of black citizens? Moreover, as the courts retreat from the effort to bring about change, the conflict seems even more pressing. Still, we go on as though it all somehow makes sense.

Our ability to make intellectually coherent and tolerable this apparent conflict is largely a product of a rhetoric that bears a distinct family resemblance to that of the nineteenth century. Like the earlier body of argument, our version helps smooth over the apparent inconsistency between our realities and our principles; it also expresses our version of the theme of white innocence and uses the rhetorical tool of abstraction.

There was a time when we might have supposed that we would not have had to face such a conflict at the close of the twentieth century. That time was the mid-1950s, and the case was *Brown v. Board of Education*.[24] *Brown* changed much and held the promise of more, yet one can see in this landmark case both the promise and the specter of what was to come by discerning both changes and continuities in the rhetoric of race.

Brown v. Board of Education, decided in 1954, was a moment of transition. With its declaration that racial segregation in schools violated the Fourteenth Amendment's guarantee of equal protection, it dramatically changed constitutional law and set off a firestorm of controversy about the institutional role of the Court that is still raging today.

The case also embodied a transition in the legal language and rhetoric of race. The advocates for racial segregation brought to the Court a chain of argument that advanced the following propositions: (1) blacks were not harmed by segregation (if anything, they were its beneficiaries); (2) whites had no reason to apologize or feel ashamed; and (3) the white person's felt need for segregation ought be respected, and, if integration were to come, it must be accomplished with careful attention to the potential harm to whites.

The legal champions of segregation, the lawyers for the Southern states, came to the Court, like the Chevalier Bayard, "without sin or reproach." The attorney general of Virginia, J. Lindsay Almond, argued:

> They are asking you to disturb the unfolding evolutionary process of education where from the dark days of the depraved institution of slavery, with the help and the sympathy and the love and the respect of the white people of the South, the colored man has risen under that educational process to a place of eminence and respect throughout this nation. It has served him well.[25]

From North Carolina came I. Beverly Lake, arguing:

> I speak on behalf of a State which is conscious of no wrongdoing in this matter. North Carolina is proud of her record in the field of Negro education. Today North Carolina is, in fact, educating more Negro children than any other state in the Union. And she is educating them well. [26]

His Texas counterpart, John Ben Shepperd, repeated the theme of paternalism and the moral virtue of the segregationist:

> There is no *discrimination* on the part of the State of Texas in administering its public school system, only *separation* of the races. It is the belief of the people of this State that discrimination against the individual can best be eliminated by segregation of the races in the educational system. It is the evil of discrimination and not segregation per se that is condemned by the United States Constitution. [27]

Shepperd pleaded for the Court's sensitivity to "the individual rights, mores and beliefs of the Southern people." [28] And he closed with a threat:

> Compulsion can only arouse resentment, individual discrimination, and, as experience has demonstrated in other states, violence. The objectives reached by the War between the States left a scar of bitterness and resentment that is visible even now in some parts of the South. Such, we hope, will not be the result of this Court's May 17th decision. [29]

Each of these men argued the innocence of the white and the absence of harm to the black.

The segregationists were also adamant in their denial of any racist motives. The lawyer for North Carolina spoke of a mysterious nonracist phenomenon, "race consciousness":

[E]verybody in North Carolina — practically everybody in North Carolina — is either Anglo-Saxon or Negro. As a result of that, we have more consciousness of race in North Carolina than is to be found in some of the border and northern states. That race consciousness is not race prejudice. It is not race hatred. It is not intolerance. It is a deeply ingrained awareness of a birthright held in trust for posterity.[30]

The Texas attorney general assured the Court, "Texas loves its Negro people and Texas will solve their problems its own way."[31]

The star of the segregationist advocates was John W. Davis. Davis was a famous lawyer who had often appeared before the Supreme Court on behalf of various causes.[32] The justices listened with virtually no interruptions to his oral argument as he defended the constitutionality of racial segregation in the public schools. With an elegant brutality, Davis argued:

You say that [segregation is a product of] racism. Well, it is not racism. Recognize that for sixty centuries and more humanity has been discussing questions of race and race tension, not racism. Say that we make special provisions for the aboriginal Indian population of this country; it is not racism. Say that 29 states have miscegenation statutes now in force which they believe are of beneficial protection to both races. Disraeli said, "No man," said he, "will treat with indifference the principle of race. It is the key of history."[33]

He concluded his oral argument thus:

Let me say this for the State of South Carolina. . . . It is confident of its good faith and intention to produce equality for all of its children of whatever race or color. It is convinced that the happiness, the progress and the welfare of these children is best promoted in segregated schools, and it thinks it a thousand pities that by this controversy there should be urged the return to an experiment which gives no more promise of success today than when it was written into their Constitution during what I call the tragic era [i.e., Reconstruction].[34]

Davis's rhetoric, and the rhetoric of the other segregationist lawyers, expressed a form of white innocence and used a form of abstraction to deny the realities of oppression. The segregationist
rhetoricians insisted on the absence of racism as a motive. Southern
whites did not harbor prejudice, hatred, or intolerance for blacks,
only "race consciousness." The segregated school system had served
black children well. The only victims on the horizon were the
whites who might be compelled to give up a way of life without
good reason. This benign picture of school segregation could be advanced only by an abstract depiction of the context. It made no
sense to say that racism was absent from the explanation for the
segregation laws once one considered these laws in any real social
or historical context. The undeniable message of segregation was
the supposed racial inferiority of blacks. To assert that blacks were
not harmed by segregated school systems seems ludicrous when
one examines the history of separate but outrageously unequal
education. Moreover, even if one pretended that the educational
facilities were equal, black children would surely have received the
message of inferiority — what else can we suppose the black children being bused many miles across Texas to a black school, passing
along the way the schools for white children, were thinking and
feeling?

The most eloquent response to the segregationists was that of
Thurgood Marshall, then appearing before the Court on behalf of
the appellants. Marshall spoke thus:

They can't take race out of this case. . . .

. . . [T]he only way that this Court can decide this case in opposition
to our position is that there must be some reason which gives the state
the right to make a classification . . . and we submit the only way to
arrive at this decision is to find that for some reason Negroes are inferior
to all other human beings. . . . The only [explanation] is an inherent
determination that the people who were formerly in slavery, regardless

of anything else, shall be kept as near that stage as is possible; and now is the time, we submit, that this Court should make it clear that that is not what our Constitution stands for.[35]

Marshall insisted that segregation was by its nature an expression of an ideology of racial inferiority and a product of just such racist motives. He denied the innocence of the white segregationist and argued the palpable harm to the stigmatized black person. Marshall knew well the recurring argument of white innocence and the use of abstraction as a rhetorical device, and he met them head on.

The Supreme Court embraced Marshall's vision of terrible harm to black children: "To separate [school children] from others of similar age and qualifications solely because of their race generates a feeling of inferiority as to their status in the community that may affect their hearts and minds in a way unlikely ever to be undone."[36] This move represented the promise of a change, not only in constitutional law but also in the legal rhetoric of race.

The other important feature of the *Brown* opinion was the Court's treatment of the rhetorical theme of white innocence. On this issue, it offered a howling silence. The Court spoke not at all of the racist motives for segregation and thus left standing the segregationists' insistence upon white innocence.

This is important to an understanding of the history of the rhetoric of race. Chief Justice Earl Warren, considered to be the architect of the *Brown* decision, had pragmatic reasons to maintain this silence. The cost of an explicit charge of racist motives would have been, at the very least, the loss of unanimity in the *Brown* decision; the price of unanimity was in effect the preservation of the concept of white innocence. In this sense, *Brown* was both a moment of transition and a moment of continuity. Abstraction from social context was rejected; "white innocence" was left intact.

We cannot know what would have been different had the Court

explicitly rejected white innocence. We can see, however, the connection between this concept and the next move the Court made.

Having concluded that segregated schools violated the constitutional rights of black families, the Court had to decide what to do about it. In an unusual move, the Court invited another round of arguments on the question of appropriate remedy. On this issue, Thurgood Marshall's position was simple and powerful. Beyond any brief time period necessary to put the machinery of desegregation into effect, he saw no basis for further delay: once the Court found that the constitutional rights of the black families were being violated, the Court's duty was to vindicate the families' rights and to order the desegregation of the public schools. The segregationists' lawyers, of course, argued for gradual — if not glacially paced — remedies.

After hearing this round of argument, the Court, in what came to be known as the *Brown II* opinion, sent the cases back to the lower federal courts with the instruction to proceed as those lower courts deemed necessary to bring about desegregation "with all deliberate speed." Thus the black families who had brought suit left the Supreme Court without a direct judicial command that their children be admitted to the white schools. The Court thereby left the actual implementation of its abstract pronouncement to the individual Southern federal judges, many of whom had no interest in aggressive, prompt enforcement. This choice of remedy facilitated the foot-dragging, dilatory strategies of the segregationists, strategies that would assure that Marshall's vision of integrated public schools would never be realized.

Undoubtedly, powerful and pragmatic arguments were advanced to support the "with all deliberate speed" remedy. The Court's abstract assertion that school segregation violated the federal Constitution was itself controversial and divisive. This assertion overruled the constitutional principle of "separate but equal." Lawyers and legal academics railed against the constitutional interpretation of the *Brown* opinion. The Court may have rightfully imagined that to compound the controversy by directly ordering the immediate desegregation of the schools would be too much, too soon. After all, John Ben Shepperd, the attorney general of Texas, had reminded the Court of the threat of violence that attended any disruption of the established ways of apartheid.

Yet, whether pragmatically justified or not, the implicit backdrop of white innocence helped to make the delay in implementation seem intellectually and socially tolerable. Had the Court in the first *Brown* opinion spoken of the racism that motivated the segregation laws, the delay in *Brown II* would have been more difficult to justify. To permit some period of time for families to adjust to a new way of life is one thing; to permit racists a period of continued expression of their racism out of fear of their resistance and lawlessness is quite another.

The Contemporary Rhetoric of Race

An analysis of the rhetoric of our contemporary cases on race reveals that the promise of *Brown* was not to be fulfilled. Much has changed. Legal apartheid is no more. Still, a generation after *Brown*, we live in an essentially segregated society, our current law provides no real basis for change, and the rhetoric of race looks more and more like its nineteenth-century counterpart.

To support the last of these sad conclusions, I have chosen three cases for analysis: *Milliken v. Bradley*,[37] *City of Memphis v. Greene*,[38] and *City of Richmond v. J. A. Croson Co.*[39] These cases span the past quarter-century, and each is an important chapter in the story of race and the Constitution. They reveal in especially powerful ways the contemporary legal rhetoric of race.

Milliken *and the End of the Promise*

In the 1974 case *Milliken v. Bradley*, the Court faced the question of whether the Constitution empowered federal courts to order interdistrict busing to achieve racial integration in the Detroit public schools. Detroit exemplified the emerging housing pattern in metropolitan areas: black inner cities and white suburbs. This housing pattern, coupled with the structure of community-based district school systems, created de facto segregation of the public schools throughout metropolitan Detroit. In such a metropolitan area, the only remedy that could bring about school desegregation was interdistrict busing. Yet a majority of the Court, in an opinion written by Chief Justice Burger, concluded that the Constitution virtually precluded this remedy.

Milliken thus represented the end of the promise of *Brown* for public school integration. Once *Milliken* functionally took away from the federal courts the power to order interdistrict busing to implement desegregation, the common pattern of de facto housing segregation in most parts of this country assured de facto segregation in the schools. Other important school desegregation cases would follow *Milliken*, but the basic principles of the case assured the eventual demise of school busing to achieve racial integration.

A central part of Burger's argument was his assertion that the suburban school districts were not perpetrators. These school districts had not committed a racially discriminatory act; they had simply provided public education to the people who lived within their communities, communities which happened to be virtually all-white. In Burger's words, "[There was] no showing of significant violation by the 53 outlying school districts and no evidence of any interdistrict violation. . . . To approve the remedy ordered by the court would impose on the outlying districts, not shown to have committed any constitutional violation, a wholly impermissible remedy based on a standard not hinted at in *Brown I* or *Brown II* or any holding of this Court."[40]

This "perpetrator perspective" is a manifestation of both the theme of white innocence and the tool of abstraction from context. The reality of the *Milliken* case, which even Burger acknowledged, was the existence of a virtually all-black inner-city school system and a virtually all-white suburban school system in metropolitan Detroit.[41] However, Burger insisted that this was not something for which the suburban whites bore any responsibility; thus to impose the remedy of busing upon them would be a victimization of innocents.

This all makes sense so long as we ignore several pieces of the story. Burger chose not to discuss the real social context in which the case arose and the social phenomena that accounted for the de facto segregation, most significantly, the phenomenon of "white flight." Prior to the enforcement of the dictates of *Brown*, the city of Detroit had constructed and maintained a segregated dual school system. When the courts compelled Detroit to integrate its school system, the white citizens of the city began leaving for the suburbs, and white families moving into the Detroit metropolitan area also clustered in these suburbs. The suburban schools became white, the city schools black, not by happenstance but through a complex set of private and public choices. Burger's line of argument obscured the reality of white flight, thereby suggesting that the segregation of suburban school districts was serendipitous or somehow mysterious. This rhetorical move preserved the non-perpetrator status of the suburban school districts. It also raised doubts about the victim status of the black school children locked into the segregated city system. After all, if this pattern of segregation just happened, no one is to blame, no one is a victim.

When one acknowledges the phenomenon of white flight as the central part of the explanation of the existence of the all-white suburban schools, the matter of innocence and victimization becomes more complex. White flight does not automatically make all whites guilty nor does it establish the victimization of the black children; it does suggest, however, that the perpetrator perspective operates at a level of abstraction that obscures the complexity of de facto school segregation.

Burger's opinion thus offered a contemporary example of the theme of white innocence, and the rhetorical move to ignore or obscure the real social context in which these stories are played out is similar to the use of abstraction in *Plessy* and *The Civil Rights Cases*.

A tragic irony is that the Court in *Milliken* undid the promise of *Brown v. Board of Education* through an opinion whose central rhetorical piece — the refusal to speak of the racism present in the social context — can be seen as a crucial flaw in Warren's opinion in *Brown*.

The Wall in Memphis

Once upon a time, two neighborhoods existed beside each other in the city of Memphis. One neighborhood, called Hein Park, was all-white, a situation first established by a set of racial covenants that precluded the sale of any property to anyone of another race. After the legal demise of such covenants, private understandings maintained the exclusive character of Hein Park. To the north of Hein Park was a black neighborhood; to the south of Hein Park was downtown Memphis. This created the unfortunate problem. Black people living nearby insisted on driving through Hein Park on their way downtown. The whites feared the threat to "the safety and tranquility" of their neighborhood presented by the passage of black motorists and asked the city to build a wall in the form of a traffic barrier between the neighborhoods. The city did so. The outraged black residents sued the city.

The case reached the Supreme Court in 1981 as *City of Memphis v. Greene*. A majority of the Court concluded that the city's decision to erect the traffic barrier violated neither the Constitution nor the applicable federal statutes. Justice Stevens devoted the bulk of his majority opinion to a characterization of the closing of the street in question as the product of a concern for safety and traffic, and not an act based on any notions of racism. He summarized the "critical facts" thus:

The city's decision to close West Drive was motivated by its interest in protecting the safety and tranquility of a residential neighborhood. The procedures followed in making the decision were fair and were not affected by any racial or other impermissible factors.[42]

Stevens relied on the city's repeated expression of the nonracial factors and the absence of any expression by city officials of any racist basis in their decision to construct the barrier.

Thurgood Marshall, the advocate for the black children and families in *Brown v. Board of Education*, had by this time become the first black Supreme Court justice. Writing in dissent, he had a different sense of the critical facts:

> First, as the District Court found, Hein Park "was developed well before World War II as an exclusive residential neighborhood for white citizens and these characteristics have been maintained." . . . Second, the area to the north of Hein Park, like the "undesirable traffic" that Hein Park wants to keep out, is predominantly Negro. And third, the closing of West Drive stems entirely from the efforts of residents of Hein Park.[43]

These facts, "combined with a dab of common sense," revealed to Marshall the racism at work in the *Memphis* case.[44]

Stevens and Marshall looked at the same case and saw two different stories. Stevens saw no racism, just residents worried about excessive traffic. Marshall saw something else. The key, again, for the majority was the absence of perpetrators, the vision of white innocence. Stevens looked only at the formal declarations of the city officials. Marshall, by contrast, focused on the story of the development of Hein Park and the history of race relations in Memphis.

The *Memphis* case contains an even stronger echo of nineteenth-century rhetoric. Stevens concluded his opinion with a civics lesson on the burdens of citizenship, directed at the black residents of Memphis.

Because urban neighborhoods are so frequently characterized by a common ethnic or racial heritage, a regulation's adverse impact on a particular neighborhood will often have a disparate effect on an identifiable ethnic or racial group. To regard an inevitable consequence of that kind as a form of stigma so severe as to violate the Thirteenth Amendment would trivialize the great purpose of that charter of freedom. Proper respect for the dignity of the residents of any neighborhood requires that they accept the same burdens as well as the same benefits of citizenship regardless of their racial or ethnic origin.[45]

Thus, in Stevens's vision, when the blacks who brought suit objected to the street closing, they objected to carrying the ordinary burdens of citizenship. Recall the civics lesson that Justice Bradley delivered to the blacks in the late nineteenth century, in *The Civil Rights Cases*: "When a man has emerged from slavery . . . there must be some stage . . . when he takes the rank of a mere citizen, and ceases to be the special favorite of the laws." Stevens also suggested, in effect, that any felt sense of stigma was constitutionally trivial and in any event was a product of the black person's misunderstanding of the nature of the governmental action. This is an echo of the argument in *Plessy* that the blacks misunderstood the message of de jure segregation and simply "imagined" a message of racial inferiority in the laws. Then and now, the Court casts African Americans as persons seeking special favor or as thin-skinned persons who imagine stigma where none exists.

Bakke, Richmond, *and the Innocent White Victim*

Today, the invocation of the innocent white victim is most evident as a central element of the argument against affirmative action — the issue that, more than any other, has been a lightning rod for contemporary race relations. The rhetoric of innocence in the affirmative action debate takes two related forms. First, the opponents of affirmative action argue the plight of the so-called innocent victims of affirmative action. The white applicant to medical school, the white contractor seeking city construction contracts, and so on, are each innocent in a particular sense of that word. Their innocence is a presumed feature, not the product of any actual and particular inquiry. It is presumed, for example, that the white contractor passed over for the city construction contract is not guilty of any specific and racist act in the past that would have shut out minority applicants; we simply assume that, whatever the disadvantages suffered in the past by minority contractors, a given white contractor was not an actor in any past racist-inspired lockout and is therefore "innocent."

The opponent of affirmative action usually avoids altogether questions that suggest a different and more complex conception of these matters. Most importantly, the rhetoric of innocence avoids the argument that white people generally have benefited from the oppression of people of color in a myriad of obvious and less obvious ways. Returning to the construction industry example, all white-owned contracting companies have arguably benefited in the past from a de facto barrier to entry by black-owned potential competitors.

The second and related part of the rhetoric of innocence in the affirmative action debate is the assertion that the black beneficiary is not a real victim. Because an affirmative action plan does not require particular and individualized proof of discrimination, its beneficiaries, it can be argued, are not necessarily victims of racial discrimination.

These two parts work as a unitary argument, as a "one-two punch." Within this rhetoric, affirmative action plans have two important effects: they hurt innocent white people and they advantage undeserving black people. Affirmative action does not merely do bad things to good white people ("good" as in "innocent"), nor does it merely do good things for bad black people ("bad" as in "undeserving"); affirmative action does both at once and in coordination. Given the obvious power of the rhetoric of innocence, its use and persistence in the debate is not surprising.

This two-part argument has figured prominently in the U.S. Supreme Court's opinions in the important affirmative action cases, beginning with *Board of Regents v. Bakke*, decided in 1978.[46] In *Bakke*, the Court struck down a medical school admissions program that set aside a specific number of places for minorities only. The majority concluded that although the admissions process might take account of race, the quota system employed by the state medical school violated the constitutional rights of white applicants.

Justice Powell introduced the rhetoric of innocence into the Court's affirmative action discourse. He wrote of the patent unfairness of "innocent persons . . . asked to endure [deprivation as] the price of membership in the dominant majority" and of "forcing innocent persons . . . to bear the burdens of redressing grievances not of their making."[47] In a passage that embodies both strands of the argument, Powell made a distinction between the case at hand and the school desegregation cases and other precedents in which racially drawn remedies were endorsed.

> The State certainly has a legitimate and substantial interest in ameliorating, or eliminating where feasible, the disabling effects of identified discrimination. The line of school desegregation cases, commencing with *Brown*, attests to the importance of this state goal and the commitment of the judiciary to affirm all lawful means toward its attainment. In the school cases, the States were required by court order to redress the wrongs worked by specific instances of racial discrimination. That goal was far more focused than the remedying of the effects of "societal discrimination," an amorphous concept of injury that may be ageless in its reach into the past.[48]

Thus Powell sought to circumscribe tightly the ambit of affirmative action.

In contrast to Powell's opinion, the dissenting opinions in *Bakke* authored by Justice Brennan and Justice Marshall each challenged the premises of this rhetoric. Brennan rejected the idea of requiring proof of individual and specific discrimination as a prerequisite to affirmative action. Marshall attacked directly the rhetoric of white innocence and the questioning of black victimization: "It is unnecessary in 20th century America to have individual Negroes demonstrate that they have been the victims of racial discrimination; the racism of our society has been so pervasive that none, regardless of wealth or position, has managed to escape its impact."[49]

The rhetoric of white innocence persisted in the language of the Court's majority opinions in the affirmative action cases following *Bakke*, and reached a crescendo in the important 1989 case *City of Richmond v. J. A. Croson Co.* The Court concluded in *Richmond* that the city's set-aside of thirty percent of the subcontracting work on city construction jobs for minority-owned firms violated the constitutional rights of white contractors. For the first time the Court applied "strict scrutiny" to an affirmative action program, thus placing affirmative action in the same constitutional domain with the apartheid laws. Other affirmative action cases would follow *Richmond*, but this represented the turning point for the constitutional status of affirmative action.

In her opinion for the Court, Justice O'Connor rejected the premise of racial discrimination in the construction industry in Richmond, Virginia. She labeled the city council's premises as "generalized assertions" and "amorphous claims," dismissing the fact that in a city whose residents were approximately fifty percent black the city's construction work virtually never went to minority-owned firms.

Justice Scalia's concurring opinion was especially impassioned in its expression of the doctrine of white innocence. He spoke of the white victims of affirmative action. When we implement affirmative action "we play with fire," warned Scalia. He warned of those who might seek to "even the score" and in other ways suggested that whites might suffer unjustly at the hands of blacks. He reminded the reader that the majority of members of the Richmond City Council were black. In sounding this warning, Scalia invited a connection with another theme of the public rhetoric of the nineteenth century — the fear of black insurrection and revenge.[50]

Thurgood Marshall dissented and focused on a different narrative. He wrote of Richmond's "disgraceful history" of race relations. Marshall told the stories of Richmond's massive resistance to school integration and its efforts to dilute the black vote, and other stories of state-sanctioned racial discrimination in Richmond. He thus tried to shift the field of argument to a more vividly depicted historical and social context. He fought against the abstraction of O'Connor and Scalia's rhetoric. Marshall concluded: "[A] majority of this Court signals that it regards racial discrimination as largely a phenomenon of the past, and that government bodies need no longer preoccupy themselves with rectifying racial injustice. I, however, do not believe this Nation is anywhere close to eradicating racial discrimination or its vestiges."[51]

In the end, in *Milliken*, *Memphis*, and *Richmond*, the Court's majority opinions made its choices intellectually tolerable through a rhetoric that bears a disturbing similarity to the rhetoric of those nineteenth-century cases we now disavow. This alone ought to make us reconsider our contemporary choices. A more careful consideration of the precise nature and cultural significance of the idea of white innocence will provide yet more reason to reconsider this line of argument and the choices it rhetorically props up.

White Innocence Revisited

To understand the power of the theme of white innocence, one must begin with the power of the cultural conception of innocence itself. To be innocent is an important thing everywhere in our culture. The very contrast between the colors white and black is often a symbol for the contrast between good and evil, innocence and defilement. Thus the theme of white innocence in the legal rhetoric of race involves more than the obvious advantage of pushing away responsibility; it draws some of its power from the cultural, religious, and sexual themes its terms suggest.

White and black often symbolize some form of good and bad. Black or darkness has been the symbol of evil for many Western cultures. Darkness is, in many Western religions, a symbol of the anti-God, and the phrase "black magic" is often used to describe a perverse form of magic or worship. In most Christian sects, darkened churches symbolize the days of Lent, while the glory of Easter is a time to throw open the windows and let in the light.

The sexual connotations of white innocence are many and complex. Put simply, innocence as chastity is often symbolized by white; in our culture, the white wedding dress is a double symbol of the connection between white and innocence and of the significance of sexual innocence.

The stereotypical depiction of black people — especially black men — as sexually wanton is long-standing.[52] Miscegenation statutes — laws forbidding marriage between whites and blacks — expressed the idea of defilement, always accompanied by the image of the defilement of a white woman by a black man. These laws existed in many states until the Court finally declared them unconstitutional in 1967, through an opinion which, although unanimous, expressed no tone of outrage about their existence. Commentators on Southern culture have noted the recurring mythology of the black man as a large, oversexed would-be defiler of white women, as in Griffith's classic motion picture *Birth of a Nation*, which depicts the suicide of an innocent white woman seeking to avoid the touch of a black man whom Griffith portrays as a slobbering beast.[53]

This connection is still with us. The image of a black man coupled with a white woman is still so controversial that movies and television avoid it with only the rarest of exceptions, and black persons are still portrayed as oversexed and wanton.

The rhetoric of innocence in the affirmative action debate draws its greatest power from these and other sources that constitute the vein of unconscious racism that runs through each of us.

Professor Charles Lawrence has explored the concept of unconscious racism and its implications for constitutional law.[54] Lawrence introduced his sense of "unconscious racism" thus:

> Americans share a common historical and cultural heritage in which racism has played and still plays a dominant role. Because of this shared experience, we also inevitably share many ideas, attitudes, and beliefs that attach significance to an individual's race and induce negative feelings and opinions about nonwhites. To the extent that this cultural belief system has influenced all of us, we are all racists. At the same time, most of us are unaware of our racism. We do not recognize the ways in which our cultural experience has influenced our beliefs about race or the occasions on which those beliefs affect our actions. In other words, a large part of the behavior that produces racial discrimination is influenced by unconscious racial motivation.[55]

Lawrence's thesis is especially disturbing to the contemporary white person who can think of a no more offensive label than that of racist. These white Americans, whether politically liberal or conservative, typically express only disgust for the words and behavior of the white supremacists and neo-Nazis they connect with the term. Lawrence's thesis also seems hard to reconcile with the undeniable shift in public discourse over the past thirty to forty years. We rarely hear politicians and other public figures use racial epithets. Expressions of the doctrine of an inherent superiority of the white race are rare and controversial. No governor today would stand in the doorway of his state university to block the entry of African American students.

Yet, even though the public ideology has become formally non-racist, the culture continues to teach racism. The media depiction of African Americans is typically consistent with stereotypes. Public opinion surveys show a willingness by white Americans, even those who do not think of themselves as racist, to express the opinion that blacks are more violence-prone, less hardworking, and less patriotic than their white counterparts. The dearth of African Americans in positions that we associate with character, judgment, and intelligence reinforces such opinions. Perhaps most importantly, the complex set of individual and collective choices that make our schools, our neighborhoods, our workplaces, and our lives racially segregated is likely to teach white children that blacks are different and to be avoided.

Racism today is at once inconsistent with the dominant public ideology and embedded in each of us, albeit for many of us at the unconscious level. This paradox of irrationality and normalcy is part of the reason for the unconscious nature of the racism: when our culture teaches us racism and our ideology teaches us that racism is evil, we respond by excluding the forbidden lesson from our consciousness.

The repression of racism is critical to the rhetoric of innocence. First, whites can sensibly claim the mantle of innocence only by denying the charge of racism; as nonracists, we have done no harm and do not deserve to suffer for the sins of the generations who preceded us. Second, the black beneficiaries of affirmative action can be denied "actual victim" status only if we think of racists as either ghosts from a distant past or aberrant and isolated characters in contemporary culture. Either way, the power of racism is minimal. Thus whites make coherent their self-conception of innocence and make it sensible to question the actual victimization of blacks.

The existence of unconscious racism undermines the idea of the "innocent white victim" and makes problematic the "victim" part of the characterization. A victim is one who suffers an undeserved loss. If the white person who is disadvantaged by an affirmative action plan is also a racist, albeit at an unconscious level, the question becomes more complicated.

The implications of unconscious racism for the societal distribution of burdens and benefits also undermine the "innocent" status of whites. As blacks are burdened in a myriad of ways because of the persistence of unconscious racism, whites are thereby benefited. For example, on a racially integrated law faculty, if a black law professor must overcome widespread assumptions of inferiority held by students and colleagues, his or her white colleagues enjoy the benefit of a positive presumption.

Interestingly, the critics of affirmative action do acknowledge this burden, but they call it a "stigma" produced by the very institution of affirmative action. Remove affirmative action to "create a level playing field" and the stigma disappears, say the critics. However, presumptions about racial inferiority predated affirmative action and will survive its dismantling. The actual consequence of dismantling affirmative action will be fewer African Americans in our colleges, in the professions, and in other places of status, and this absence of black faces will only reinforce our unconscious racism. This will be the legacy of the abandonment of affirmative action, not the promised eradication of stigma.

The historical manifestations of racism have worked to the advantage of whites, undoubtedly. Just as slavery provided the resources to make possible the genteel life of the plantation owner and his white family in early nineteenth-century Virginia, more than a century later that state's system of segregation in public schools and the state university diverted the state's resources to me and not to my black peers. The obvious advantages of the state-sponsored racism that persisted until almost thirty years ago in this country, the benefits of which are still being reaped by whites today, are not the only basis for skewing the societal balance sheet. Racist cultural teachings persist, and unconscious racism continues to operate to the disadvantage of blacks and to the advantage of whites today. In job interviews and social encounters, in courtrooms and conference rooms, and on the streets, the presence and power of unconscious racism is apparent. In our culture, where most Americans at a conscious or unconscious level see blacks as lazy, dumb, and prone to crime, blacks are burdened and whites are correspondingly advantaged.

The critic of affirmative action often seeks at once to acknowledge and to belittle the power of racism by declaring that mere "societal discrimination" is an insufficient predicate for affirmative action. "Societal discrimination" suggests an ephemeral, abstract kind of discrimination, committed by no one in particular (the "society" discriminates) and committed against no one in particular, a kind of amorphous inconvenience for persons of color. By using this term, the white rhetorician can at once acknowledge the existence of racism and, by giving it a different name, give it a different and trivial connotation.

Yet, when we recall just how many important choices are made by reference to inherently subjective standards, the specter of societal discrimination does not seem a trivial inconvenience. Hiring, selecting with whom one does business, bestowing awards, voting in political races, and so on, are all such decisions.

The rhetoric of innocence and unconscious racism connect in yet another way. The rhetoric draws power from its embodiment of the basic tenets of racism. Blacks are, according to the deepest racist stereotype, lazy, dirty, and oversexed. The "dirty and oversexed" piece of racism makes the black beneficiary of affirmative action a "defiled taker," the perfect implicit, and unconsciously embraced, contrast to the innocent white victim of affirmative action. The use of the idea of innocence and its opposite, defilement, coalesces with the unconscious racist belief that the black person is not innocent in a sexual sense, that black people are sexually defiled by promiscuity.

Similarly, the "lazy" part of racism gives the rhetoric of innocence power. When Senator Jesse Helms of North Carolina ran
against Harvey Gantt, an African American, Helms used an anti-
affirmative action ad that showed a pair of black hands taking a slip
of paper representing a job. The text of the ad stressed the plight of
the innocent white victim. Surely this ad would have had a powerful
impact on any white North Carolina voter who had actually lost a
job or promotion to an affirmative action candidate. Yet, outside of
government workplaces, universities, and certain large institutional employers, affirmative action policies are not the norm and,
when in place, are often toothless pronouncements. Most white
Americans, in North Carolina or elsewhere, have not in fact lost a
job or promotion to a black candidate, so Helms's ad was surely
aimed at a larger segment of the white audience. The ad drew its
larger measure of power from its invocation of the anger and resent-
ment so many whites feel at the image of the undeserving black person of the racist stereotype, who seeks and takes the unearned advantage of affirmative action.

The point is not that everyone who argues for the innocent white
victims of affirmative action is consciously drawing on stereotypical
racist images. Nor is every member of the white audience consciously embracing those racist beliefs when they experience the
rhetoric of innocence in affirmative action discourse. Many of the
rhetoricians and much of their audience are likely to reject stereotypes at the conscious level; moreover, they would be offended at
the very suggestion that they might be racists. Yet these beliefs are
still there, even in the white liberal, because the teacher is our culture, and any person who is part of that culture has been taught the
lesson of racism. While many of us have struggled to unlearn it and
have succeeded at the conscious level, few of us can slough off racism
altogether at the unconscious level.

Ironically, the rhetoric of white innocence is arguably more powerful than ever. Our public ideology and discourse is ostensibly

nonracist. Judges cannot say out loud that blacks are inferior. Lawyers cannot make arguments with the explicit premises of racism.
However, when the contemporary rhetoric of white innocence invites the cultural connections and images of the past, we tap into a
repressed vein of unconscious racism which is difficult to challenge
because it is expressed indirectly and metaphorically.

When we see that our legal rhetoric of race is filled with the idea
of white innocence and the device of abstracting argument from social context, we have reason to doubt that our choices are any better
than the nineteenth-century choices that stain our legal history.
The rhetorical tools that helped make coherent the despicable legal
choices of the nineteenth century continue to serve in contemporary
legal choices about race. Yet we purchase our comfort by refusing
to take seriously the conscious and unconscious racism that pervades our culture, and by proclaiming our innocence.

Like the Southern white man of a century and a half ago, we
imagine that we stand without sin and without reproach before the
judgment of history and God. I fear that God and history will
judge otherwise.

3

Their Immorality,
Our Helplessness

Poor people are different from the rest of us. Most of them are morally weak and undeserving. And in any event we are helpless to solve the complex and daunting problem of poverty. This is the rhetoric of poverty.

The U.S. Supreme Court has addressed the constitutional claims of poor people in a range of contemporary cases, and the rhetoric of poverty runs through these opinions. Poor people, it is said or implied, are unwilling to work and especially likely to commit fraud and child abuse, or to violate other legal and moral norms. They have bad attitudes and are the cause of their own poverty. At the same time, the problem of poverty is, in this rhetoric, a problem of daunting complexity that is virtually beyond solution.

These themes as seen in context of actual Supreme Court cases are either shamefully inapt or, at the least, problematic. When we see that the Court's choices are shored up by this sort of rhetorical structure, we shall have good reason to question those choices.

The first step, the creation of the abstraction "the poor," is an easily overlooked yet powerful part of the rhetoric of poverty. We are so used to speaking of the poor as a distinct class that we forget the rhetorical significance of doing so. By focusing on the single variable of economic wealth and then drawing a line on the wealth continuum, we create a class of people who are "them," not us. Creating this abstraction is, in one sense, merely a way of speaking. After all, we must resort to categories and abstractions in order to discuss large issues sensibly. Moreover, there is a meaningful difference between the circumstances of a family in poverty and a middle-class family, and to ignore these real differences can lead to injustice. Thus, to speak of "the poor" is a sensible way to talk. In the rhetorical context of the law, however, it is much more.

The creation of any category of people makes it possible to generalize about their moral worth as a conceptually distinct group. Within our culture we have always thought of the poor as morally weak, even degenerate. Thus, in dialogue about the plight of the poor, we are likely to hear the message that we are normal, "they" are deviant. Our feelings about this range from empathy to violent hatred. Still, even in the most benevolent view, the poor are seen as different. Their deviance is a product of a single aspect of their lives, their relative wealth position, and all other aspects of their lives are either ignored or seen through this lens. By creating this division and consequent class of people, we are able at once to distinguish "us" from "them" and to appropriate normalcy to our own lives and circumstances.

The assertion of judicial helplessness is also connected to widely shared and longstanding cultural assumptions about the nature of poverty, starting with the assumption that poverty is somehow built into the basic structure of our society. We assume that the eradication of poverty, even if possible in theory, would require the radical transformation of society itself. The causes of poverty, it is said, are a product of a complex set of factors tied to politics, culture, history, psychology, and philosophy; thus only in a radically different world might poverty cease to exist. And whatever the extent of the powers of the Court, radically remaking the world is not one of them.

These dual themes of their moral deviance and our helplessness seem at first to be inconsistent. The premise of moral weakness suggests that the problem is really quite simple. If poor people simply chose to "straighten up and fly right," all would be well. If they would accept and commit to the moral norms of those not in poverty, they would cease to be poor, albeit only after a long time and much hard work. In this vision of poverty, the problem is one-dimensional and it is intractable only to the extent that poor people resist the personal, individual reform of their moral lives. The helplessness theme, on the other hand, most often depends on the idea of the complexity of the problem and on the existence of multiple, intertwined causes. Despite this apparent inconsistency, the justices-rhetoricians use both themes throughout, and often in tandem, in their opinions.

This apparent inconsistency in the Court's rhetoric of poverty may be related to yet another enduring cultural assumption, the division of the poor into the classes of deserving and undeserving poor. These classes have been drawn somewhat differently at different points in history. The contemporary division is between able-bodied adults, on the one hand, and the children, aged, and disabled, on the other. The distinction is premised on the ability of the former class to perform work.

We need two different explanations for our helplessness for these two different classes. For the undeserving poor, we can say that the cause of their poverty is their moral weakness, a matter beyond our control. For the deserving poor, we can say instead that the institution of poverty is too complex and multifaceted for us to undo. The dual rhetoric of moral weakness and judicial helplessness fits the needs of a society and a legal system that have chosen to minimize intervention on behalf of the poor. Either the poor do not deserve intervention, or, if they are innocent, we are functionally helpless to lift them out of their plight.

The rhetorician builds an argument out of the available cultural assumptions and attitudes. The premise of the moral weakness of the poor has been around in various forms for centuries, the argument that we are helpless to change the harsh reality of persons in poverty has a long lineage in American public discourse, and the particular argument of judicial helplessness has served as the rhetorical linchpin for important legal issues throughout our legal history, most notably in matters of race and poverty. To understand the nature and the power of the contemporary legal rhetoric of poverty requires some understanding of the history and cultural standing of its basic premises.

"Us" and "Them"

In our culture and most other Western cultures, in one fashion or another, the poor have always been separated by class distinctions and labels. They have been our "paupers," "peasants," and "strangers." They have been cast as different, deviant, and morally weak.

Just as the separation and stigmatization of the poor has been a recurring cultural assumption, the intensified suffering of the poor in hard times has been a recurring reality. During the great plagues of Europe, for example, the poor were left in what became ghettos of disease and death, while the affluent fled for enclaves outside the cities; the plagues took the lives of a much larger percentage of the poor than of the affluent. The stories of famine, wars, and natural disasters followed a similar pattern, with the burdens falling disproportionately on the poor. Historically, cultural assumptions both cause and help make coherent the physical separation and disproportionate suffering of the poor.

The particular assumptions about the poor have varied greatly across cultures and time. It would be comforting to suppose that we have essentially sloughed off these historical themes. Although we obviously have not banished poverty from the cultural landscape, we would like to think that our assumptions about poor people are not anything like the assumptions of our European ancestors who walled the poor into the plague-ridden urban ghettos. Yet throughout this country's history the poor have been distinguished from those not in poverty and have been the subject of moral censure.

In eighteenth-century America, the law typically imposed some responsibility on each community to assist its own poor. Poor people found within the boundaries of the community but not recognized as its members were sent back to their own towns or villages. Communities expended many resources in shunting poor people out of their midst and in resisting the claims of outsiders.

Many American communities in the late eighteenth and early nineteenth centuries concluded that even the burden of providing assistance to their own needy members had become too great. The problem, they were convinced, was the able-bodied — and hence undeserving — recipient of public assistance. The solution was to purge these undeserving poor persons from the system of public assistance. To do so required that the community make a distinction between the deserving and the undeserving poor, one that remains etched to this day in our cultural and legal conceptions of poverty.

The nineteenth-century name for the undeserving poor was "paupers." The Reverend Charles Burroughs, preaching in 1834 at the opening of a chapel in a New Hampshire poorhouse, spoke of the distinction between poverty and pauperism:

> In speaking of poverty, let us never forget that there is a distinction between this and pauperism. The former is an unavoidable evil. . . . It is the result, not of our faults, but of our misfortunes. . . . Pauperism is the consequence of willful error, of shameful indolence, of vicious habits. It is a misery of human creation, the pernicious work of man, the lamentable consequence of bad principles and morals. [1]

This moral censure of the able-bodied recipient of public assistance has never left us.

The Depression, like all great social dislocations, changed somewhat the way we thought about things. The commonly held conception of the able-bodied man, unemployed and poor, was obviously affected by the experience of the Depression because of the sheer numbers of working adults who suddenly found themselves unemployed and without hope of finding work. Nonetheless, the social stigma attached to receipt of public assistance remained. Even during a time of catastrophic economic conditions, we could not shake the idea that there was something wrong about an able-bodied man receiving public assistance.

A special and enduring legacy of the Depression and the New Deal was yet another line drawn through the ranks of the poor — the distinction between "public assistance" and "social insurance."[2] Social insurance, exemplified by Social Security benefit programs for the aged and the disabled, was thought of as a form of insurance against the "natural" events that impose financial hardships on us. People who were merely poor, on the other hand, depended instead on public assistance. This distinction paid no attention to the fortuities that might have led a poor person into that status, nor did it bother much with the fact that the benefits paid out to the aged under Social Security might exceed the value of the private contributions made. This new dichotomy, social insurance versus public assistance, served to underscore the undeserved quality of the benefits extended to recipients of the latter.

The line-drawing and moral censure, at least in terms of the public and political discourse, took a brief detour in the 1960s. The establishment of many new federal programs collectively known as the War on Poverty was the product of a period of unrelenting growth in the gross national product and unbounded optimism about society's ability to abolish poverty, without any real sacrifice. During this time, much of the public discourse rejected any correlation between poverty and moral weakness. Yet, as the War on Poverty came unraveled in the wash of blood, here and in Southeast

Asia, and as people came to see the actual sacrifice entailed in eliminating poverty, the public discourse soon drifted back to the theme of moral weakness.

The rhetoric of poverty of the 1980s was exemplified by the various forms of the narrative of a black woman receiving fraudulently obtained public assistance and driving away in her Cadillac. The 1980s also saw the rise of yet another name to categorize the poor — "the underclass." As described by Ken Auletta in his book of the same name, this category included

> (a) the *passive poor*, usually long-term welfare recipients; (b) the *hostile* street criminals who terrorize most cities, and who are often school dropouts and drug addicts; (c) the *hustlers*, who, like street criminals, may not be poor and who earn their livelihood in an underground economy, but rarely commit violent crimes; (d) the *traumatized* drunks, drifters, homeless, shopping bag ladies and released mental patients who frequently roam or collapse on city streets.[3]

Immoral or socially deviant behavior determined membership in this class. The concept of the underclass etched deeper the division between the poor and the not-poor. It also connected perfectly with the rhetorical theme of moral weakness. The behavior that characterized the underclass was criminal, antisocial, or without hope or dignity. The idea of the "passive poor," beyond hope or any sense of initiative, expressed the pervasive notion that poor people were unwilling to pull themselves up by their bootstraps and were instead happy to feed at the public trough.

"The underclass" was thus a late-twentieth-century form of that historically persistent category the undeserving poor. And, like its historical antecedents, the idea seemed to be driven more by ideology than by any attempt to accurately generalize about the circumstances and nature of poverty in America. Michael Katz, the author of *In the Shadow of the Poorhouse* and *The Undeserving Poor*, contrasted the idea of the underclass with the reality:

In fact, as a metaphor, the underclass obscures more than it reveals. It glosses over differences in condition that require varied forms of help, and it passes lightly over two salient features of poverty and welfare in America: their widespread and transient character. In the Michigan study, which followed a large sample of American families for 10 years, . . . both poverty and welfare use . . . lasted relatively briefly, and children whose parents relied on welfare were no more likely to need public assistance as adults than were others in the sample. What the study shows, in short, is that poverty is more accurately perceived now, as before in American history, as a point on a continuum rather than a sharp, clearly demarcated category of social experience. In truth, the forces that push individuals and families into poverty originate in the structure of America's political economy. Some of us are lucky, not different.[4]

This "metaphor" of the underclass is the perfect expression of the rhetorical themes of difference and deviance. Perhaps because it so perfectly expresses persistent historical themes, it has been taken up in public discourse notwithstanding its metaphoric and distorting quality.

The precise content of the commonly held assumptions about people in poverty has changed throughout American history. The nineteenth-century idea of the pauper is different from the late-twentieth-century idea of the underclass. Still, there has always been an "us / them" conception of people in poverty. And we have always found ways to make "their" suffering intellectually coherent.

Our Claim of Helplessness

Observers often interweave the premise of moral weakness with the argument for the complexity of the problem of poverty. After all, if poverty is essentially a problem of moral weakness, if poor people must undergo a personal and individual transformation, what can we do to effect such change? Historically, we have often encouraged the poor to extricate themselves from poverty by making sure that its conditions are especially horrific. We are disappointed when so many poor people seem to insist on not mending their ways and, to our surprise, seem willing to remain in poverty. This disappointment in turn feeds the argument of helplessness. If poor people are unwilling to change their behavior and values in response to the strongest of incentives, the horror of life in poverty, what else can we do?

Yet our claim of helplessness in the face of poverty is problematic. Poverty arises out of the politics of distribution.⁵ In this country, we have more than enough to meet the basic needs of everyone in our society, yet we persist in speaking of poverty as though it were a problem beyond the limits of our material resources. Perhaps the persistence of poverty leads to the idea that it is somehow inherent in the structure of our society. But all that has ever been required at any moment in our history is a redistribution of wealth. A common argument against such a redistribution is that it will dull the incentives for productive work to the degree that over time we will face the problem of scarcity and poverty will arise again. Whatever the merits of this untested hypothesis, the choice not to engage in the redistribution is nonetheless a choice.

Another sort of plea for helplessness exists in the legal rhetoric of poverty. It is the special plea of judicial helplessness, which asserts that judges do not possess the power to act.

To profess powerlessness can be the most powerful of rhetorical moves. When the court acts and chooses affirmatively, the judge's argument is about the wisdom and coherence of the action taken. This form of argument invites society's consideration and acceptance. The argument of judicial helplessness, on the other hand, shuts off the debate. The court has no power to act; therefore considerations of the wisdom and utility of whatever actions might have been taken are beside the point. Normative debate is in no sense invited.

The profession of judicial helplessness is an expression of what has been called the "irony of jurisdiction."[6] A court essentially determines the perimeters of its own jurisdiction. In a governmental structure premised on multiple sources of power, each source must have some limits, and someone must draw the boundaries. In our federal system, the Supreme Court defines the limits of power of each branch of government. On a smaller scale, each judge who decides that his or her court lacks jurisdiction is defining the limits of that court's power. Thus judges are rendered helpless by their choice to be helpless.

Judges have invoked the rhetoric of judicial helplessness most fervently when confronted with a problem of unjust and tragic dimensions. In his book *Justice Accused*, Robert Cover analyzed perhaps the most evocative and tragic example of the use of the rhetoric of helplessness in our legal history, "the complicity of the antislavery judge in a system of law that he himself considered immoral."[7] Cover examined the choices and rhetoric of American judges who believed that slavery was immoral but who as judges were asked to enforce the legal structures by which slavery existed.

One of the Supreme Court justices who figured prominently in Cover's book was John McLean. Appointed in 1829, McLean participated in the Court's most important slavery decisions. Although he was utterly opposed in principle to the institution of slavery, he chose to validate the legal structures whereby slave owners might retake fugitive slaves. Everything we know about McLean as a man indicates that his abhorrence of slavery was real and deep. Still, his actions as judge were at odds with this belief. McLean explained this dissonance by the invocation of what Cover called the rhetoric of "the judicial can't." McLean wrote:

With the abstract principles of slavery, courts called to administer the law have nothing to do. It is for the people, who are sovereign, and their representatives, in making constitutions and in the enactment of laws, to consider the laws of nature, and the immutable principles of right. This is a field which judges cannot explore. . . . They look to the law, and to the law only. A disregard of this by the judicial powers, would undermine and overturn the social compact.[8]

The pertinent question, in McLean's view, was not whether slavery was moral, but instead whether judges should be guided by their morality in making their choices. McLean answered the question by putting aside his personal view of slavery and enforcing the laws that propped up the institution. Cover said of McLean, "He consistently attributed to others whatever power existed to ameliorate the situation, and he used the language of helplessness more than any other single judge."[9]

Throughout our legal history, other judges have used the rhetoric of judicial helplessness to make intellectually coherent actions that would later be seen as tragic and shameful. The 1944 decision in *Korematsu v. United States*, which validated the internment of American citizens of Japanese ancestry during World War II, provides a vivid example. Justice Frankfurter, in his concurring opinion, concluded that the internment fell within the "war power" of the executive branch and thus outside the power of the Court. He explained, "To find that the Constitution does not forbid the military measures now complained of does not carry with it approval of that which Congress and the executive did. That is their business, not ours."

Welfare and the Rhetoric of Poverty

Legal rhetoric embodies dominant cultural assumptions. When judges construct their arguments, they must depend on narratives widely shared within their audience. Judges depend on certain assumptions and the stories behind them both because they give the argument power and the potential for influence and also because the judges, as members of the culture, are likely to believe them. Thus, because the dominant nineteenth-century view was that poor people were morally degenerate, the premise of moral degeneracy of poor people was part of the legal rhetoric of the period.

The embodiment of cultural assumptions in legal rhetoric occurs in two ways: judges state them explicitly, and judges implicitly incorporate such assumptions by making arguments that invite the reader to supply them.

Our legal rhetoric is littered with examples of the explicit and implicit invocation of the premises of the rhetoric of poverty. Perhaps the now most infamous example of the Court's nineteenth-century rhetoric of poverty is the 1837 case *City of New York v. Miln*.[10] In *Miln* the Court upheld the validity of a New York statute that required the master of every ship arriving in New York to report the occupation of each passenger. Justice Barbour, writing for the Court, explained the rationality of the state statute:

> We think it as competent and as necessary for a state to provide precautionary measures against the moral pestilence of paupers . . . as it is to guard against the physical pestilence that which may arise from unsound and infectious articles imported, or from a ship, the crew of which may be laboring under an infectious disease.[11]

Legal argument has changed along with the change in dominant cultural assumptions. Blunt assertions of the moral degeneracy of poor people are less common in the twentieth century. Moreover, there was a moment in our legal history when it appeared that the rhetoric of poverty was about to be wholly reconstructed. From the late 1950s through the early 1970s, the Court decided cases that both in choice and in rhetoric expressed a new respect for the poor.

Justice Brennan, in his opinion in *Goldberg v. Kelly*, expressed this new vision of the constitutional status of poverty:

> From its founding the Nation's basic commitment has been to foster the dignity and well-being of all persons within its borders. We have come to recognize that forces not within the control of the poor contribute to their poverty. . . . Welfare, by meeting the basic demands of subsistence, can help bring within the reach of the poor the same opportunities that are available to others to participate meaningfully in the life of the community. . . . Public assistance, then, is not mere charity, but a means to "promote the general Welfare, and secure the Blessings of Liberty to ourselves and to our Posterity."[12]

In *Goldberg v. Kelly* the Court held that welfare benefits were a form of constitutionally protected "property" and thus could not be terminated without notice and the opportunity for a hearing. During this period, the Court also granted indigent criminal defendants new rights, perhaps most importantly the right to counsel, extended in the landmark 1963 case *Gideon v. Wainwright.*

The promise of change in the constitutional status of poverty, suggested by the decisions and rhetoric of *Goldberg* and other cases, has all but disappeared in the wake of the Burger, and now Rehnquist, Court. With this shift in jurisprudence has come a return to the rhetorical theme of the moral weakness of the poor.

The transfer of wealth is the most direct response to poverty, arguably the only means whereby poverty might be eliminated. In theory, the Court might have interpreted the Constitution to assure each person a basic level of subsistence, a form of economic rights to parallel the political rights that the Court has recognized. The Court might have found a constitutional right to some minimum level of material resources. This was not a realistic expectation during the Warren tenure; Justice Brennan's hint of such a possibility in *Goldberg* was as close as the Warren Court ever came to such a move. It is a move beyond imagination for the contemporary Court.

Although the Constitution has not been a source of positive rights to food, clothing, shelter, education, or other basic material necessities, the Warren Court did review and at times constrain the structure and process of public assistance. The Court used the constitutional principle that the state may not deprive anyone of "property," including public assistance, without "due process." The constitutional conception of due process has both a substantive and a procedural component. Procedurally, it mandates notice and an opportunity for a hearing before the deprivation. In its substantive version, the principle demands that any deprivation of property by the state has to have a rational basis. Thus, following the lead of *Goldberg*, the contemporary Court might have chosen to oversee wealth transfer programs to assure rationality in their basic structures and decency and fairness in their administration. This, however, has not happened. The cases chronicling the Court's choice to leave these matters to the political actors and their agents are littered with the rhetoric of poverty.

The federal Aid to Families With Dependent Children program (AFDC) has been the contemporary lightning rod for the rhetoric of poverty. This wealth transfer program, from its origins in the early part of this century, has evolved in public perception and narrative from a program for white widows to a program for black welfare mothers who, in the harshest of the stereotypical imageries, procreate irresponsibly and have no aspirations beyond maximizing their take from the public trough.[13] (The first image of the welfare recipient was roughly accurate in its time. Through the earlier part of the century, the overwhelming majority of AFDC recipients were white women. A study of AFDC published in 1931 showed 96 percent white recipients. This same study showed only one black family in the entire state of North Carolina received

AFDC. Thus AFDC in its early years did have a white face, because the state officials excluded the numerous needy black families.)

Dandridge v. Williams

In 1970 the Supreme Court rejected a challenge to Maryland's method of funding AFDC.[14] The federal AFDC law gave states some discretion in setting the level of benefits. Maryland had chosen to fund AFDC at 100 percent of calculated need, subject to a maximum grant ceiling. Once the family reached six members, they received no additional assistance, however large the family. The maximum grant that resulted from this ceiling equaled the income of a person employed full-time at the minimum wage. The state apparently did not want a welfare family receiving more than a family with an employed member. The effect of the ceiling was to ensure that families larger than six persons would receive AFDC benefits less than their acknowledged need.

In *Dandridge v. Williams*, several AFDC recipients sued to enjoin the application of the maximum grant ceiling. They argued that the regulation was in conflict with the federal statute and was also unconstitutional. The AFDC families argued that there was no legitimate and rational basis for meeting the acknowledged need of families of six or fewer persons and not meeting the need of families of more than six persons. A majority of the Court disagreed and concluded that the regulation was consistent with the statute and was sufficiently rational to survive the constitutional challenge.

Justice Stewart, writing for the majority, concluded, "It is enough that a solid foundation for the regulation can be found in the State's legitimate interest in encouraging employment and in avoiding discrimination between welfare families and the families of the working poor."[15] Most readers would find this to be a coherent idea. We understand that low levels of public assistance encourage the acceptance of minimum-wage jobs and thus help ensure the supply of cheap labor that the society needs. Moreover, we are likely to find the specter of a "welfare family" having more than a "wage earner family" disturbing. Yet how do we come to this sense of the matter?

The welfare status of a family is appropriately a basis for deciding what they deserve only if the family is somehow responsible for its status. The reader of Stewart's *Dandridge* opinion can easily think of the welfare family as responsible for its status if one concludes that the choices and behavior of the members of that family are largely responsible for their poverty. Thus Stewart's argument for an equitable balance invites the reader to a series of associations that likely lead to the specter of the welfare recipient as shirking employment, choosing to be a recipient of public assistance and not a wage earner, which is the most common contemporary version of the expression of the moral weakness of the poor.

Yet Stewart's argument for the rationality of the statute cannot be simply grounded in the need to ensure that no wage earner family is worse off than any AFDC family. After all, an eight-person family struggling on a single minimum-wage income might be worse off than a six-person AFDC family, notwithstanding the grant ceiling. The grant ceiling's most obvious effect is within the community of AFDC families — making large AFDC families worse off than smaller ones. Maryland's argument for the rationality of this acknowledged effect of the grant ceiling was that it provided "incentives for family planning."[16]

The family planning argument is a now-familiar and critical piece of the rhetoric in today's welfare reform debate. Both in the *Dandridge* case and today, it depends on a simple set of assumptions. By putting a ceiling on benefits, any mother who is at the ceiling has an incentive to avoid incurring the financial burden of another child for whom she will receive no additional benefits; the choice to have another child becomes a choice to put her entire family, already in desperate straits, in an even worse position.

The family planning argument is also a trigger for the rhetorical theme of the moral weakness of the poor. "Family planning" in this context must mean a concern for the number of children in the family, and for this argument to be coherent, the state must have a legitimate interest in limiting the number of children in AFDC families. The grant ceiling provides the incentive for the AFDC mother to stop having babies. When the argument is broken down in this fashion, the theme of deviance and moral weakness, implicit in the argument, is easier to see. For poor women, becoming pregnant is an act of moral weakness.

To see more clearly how this argument takes its power from the theme of the moral weakness of the poor, one need simply imagine the popular response to another version of this state action: if the government chose to put a ceiling on the number of dependents that could be claimed for tax purposes by wage earners, and the state defended that law's rationality as providing "incentives for family planning," the public outcry would be pervasive and impassioned. We would argue that determining the size of the family is a personal choice, beyond the state's interest. We would find the premises of the argument offensive. We suppose that if we have a child, it is the product of a deliberate and moral choice; if the child was unplanned and we are opposed to abortion, we would assert that the decision to have the child was out of our hands. [17] Most Americans would be disturbed and offended by any such state intrusion into their decisions about the size of their families.

The two contexts, of course, are not the same. Although the children of families not in poverty are subsidized by the government through various tax deductions, public school financing, and other publicly funded services, these families do not rely on government for their basic income. Still, we also see a difference in part because we do not make the same assumptions about the people involved. Because we assume that the poor are more likely to act irresponsibly, we see as appropriate and sensible the blunt use of governmental power to make AFDC mothers "plan" their families.

The strength of the family planning argument for most people depends on a combination of a simplistic set of assumptions about our system of subsidy and wealth reallocation, coupled with the implicit theme of moreal weakness. Although we strongly believe in the private and responsible nature of our own choices to have children, we simply do not see the choices of women in poverty the same way. However outraged many of us would be at the use of governmental power to make us desist from having a child or to make us abort an unplanned child, we see little problem in doing precisely that to poor women.

Stewart concluded his *Dandridge* opinion with an assertion of helplessness:

> We do not decide today that the Maryland regulation is wise, that it best fulfills the relevant social and economic objectives that Maryland might ideally espouse, or that a more just and humane system could not be devised. . . . But the intractable economic, social, and even philosphical problems presented by public welfare assistance programs are not the business of this Court. . . . [T]he Constitution does not empower this Court to second-guess state officials charged with the difficult responsibility of allocating limited public welfare funds among the myriad of potential recipients. [18]

Stewart's concluding passage is a dual message. He refers to the helplessness of the Court, its lack of the power to intervene. He also urges the practical helplessness of us all, by his reference to the "intractable economic, social, and even philosophical problems" of poverty and welfare and to the "myriad of potential recipients." In this vision, the problem of poverty and welfare is dauntingly complex and the poor simply overwhelm the finite resources available for their assistance.

Welfare and poverty pose difficult problems. But the issue in *Dandridge* was the constitutionality of Maryland's maximum grant ceiling and not whether the Court ought to declare the radical disparity in wealth that accounts for poverty to be unconstitutional. The problem in *Dandridge* was not the existence of poverty but rather the much smaller subsidiary question of whether a particular piece of the welfare structure ought to be deemed constitutionally acceptable. One can concede for the sake of argument the Court's practical impotence to abolish poverty itself and still not give away the smaller question actually posed in *Dandridge*. To be helpless to change the largest manifestations of injustice is not a logically sufficient basis for refusing to change a small component of an unjust structure.

Stewart's implicit assumption was that the Court must either be in the business of completely restructuring welfare or it must stay out of it altogether. This argument ignores the possibility that there are more than two choices that might be made. For example, in *Dandridge* the Court might have concluded that the Maryland scheme was insufficiently rational to justify the hardship it imposed on large families in poverty. By itself, this alternative choice would not have committed the Court to the seemingly impossible task of restructuring the welfare state; the Court might have committed itself to the more modest task of assuring a reasonable measure of sense and humanity within the existing system.

The majority's choice and the rhetoric of helplessness expressed in *Dandridge* were to become the choice and rhetoric of the Court's subsequent cases. Throughout this jurisprudence, the Court has professed its helplessness and has validated welfare structures that satisfy formal rationality yet lack wisdom, justice, and humanity.

Wyman v. James

The Court's rhetoric of the moral weakness of the poor has nowhere been more pronounced than in the 1971 case of *Wyman v. James*.[19] In *Wyman* the Court rejected a constitutional challenge to New York's AFDC regulations requiring AFDC recipients to submit to home visits by caseworkers as a condition of the receipt of benefits. The purpose of the visits was to check on the continuing eligibility of the family and on the well-being of the children. The regulation required no notice to the family and the visits were often undertaken without prior notice. The plaintiff in *Wyman*, Mrs. James, had been receiving AFDC benefits. She had offered to meet caseworkers in their offices or elsewhere and to provide whatever information they sought, but she refused to permit caseworkers into her home. When the state responded by cutting off her AFDC benefits, Mrs. James sued, arguing that the regulations violated her Fourth Amendment right to be free of unreasonable searches of her home.

Justice Blackmun's opinion for the majority embodied in several ways the premise of moral weakness. Blackmun quoted, without any hint of disapproval, the following passage from the regulations: "A child or minor shall be considered eligible for AFDC if his home situation is one in which his physical, mental and moral well-being will be safeguarded and his religious faith preserved and protected."[20] This moral / religious check is of course in addition to the eligibility requirements regarding material impoverishment. Putting aside the question of how the religious faith of a poor child could be a legitimate subject of inquiry for the state, the regulation is troubling because it becomes coherent only if one assumes that the state has some particular reason to monitor the "moral well-being" of poor children.

Blackmun built his analytical structure around the double-barreled argument that the home visit was not a search in the Fourth Amendment sense, and that even if it was, it was not "unreasonable." In explaining the second point, he relied on "a number of factors."

First, Blackmun cast the dispute as a conflict between the child's needs and "what the mother claims as her rights." In this way he placed the state and the child in opposition to the mother. Blackmun explained this conflict between the interests of the mother and those of the child when he asserted that the purpose of the home visit was to assure that the funds were being used for the benefit of the child and not solely for the mother's benefit. Because there was no evidence that the funds were in fact being spent in a manner contrary to the interests of the child, this assertion depends on the assumption of a propensity of the mother to act contrary to the interests of her own children. Such an assumption would offend any mother and would be unlikely to be used as a premise outside the context of welfare and poverty. For example, if the government conditioned the middle-class family's income tax deduction for dependents on unannounced home visits and explained that condition as one necessary to assure that the tax benefit was being used in the dependent's best interests, middle-class America would be up in arms. Although the two contexts are different, the underlying premise in each instance is the state's strong need to monitor the welfare of the child. This is a premise we reject, explicitly or implicitly, except when applied to the poor.

Justice Blackmun expressed the premise of moral weakness perhaps most vividly in *Wyman* through his invocation of the specter of child abuse, set up by the alignment of mother versus child described above and by the use of phrases like "possible exploitation of the child."[21] Blackmun continued:

We have examined Mrs. James' case record with the New York City Department of Social Services, which, as an exhibit, accompanied defendant Wyman's answer. It discloses numerous interviews from the time of the initial one on April 27, 1967, until the attempted termination in June 1969. The record is revealing as to Mrs. James' failure ever really to satisfy the requirements for eligibility; as to constant and repeated demands; as to attitude toward the caseworker; as to reluctance to cooperate; as to evasiveness; and as to occasional belligerency. There are indications that all was not always well with the infant Maurice (skull fracture, a dent in the head, a possible rat bite). The picture is a sad and unhappy one.[22]

Blackmun suggests in this passage that Mrs. James was physically abusing her child. But the issue in *Wyman* was whether the New York home visit regulations were constitutional, not whether Mrs. James had committed child abuse; the state had not sought to visit Mrs. James's home on the basis of any such suspicion. Thus Blackmun's suggestion seems irrelevant and gratuitous, but it becomes relevant to the constitutional issue the moment one plugs in the premise of moral weakness; the story of Mrs. James and "the infant Maurice" becomes a narrative about AFDC mothers generally and their propensity by virtue of their poverty status to abuse their children.[23] Blackmun's story then provides a state interest in home visits for the purpose of monitoring a group of parents seen as especially prone to the abuse of their children.

Blackmun's further comments about Mrs. James's "attitude" are also revealing: "What Mrs. James appears to want from the agency that provides her and her infant son with the necessities for life is the right to receive those necessities upon her own informational terms, to utilize the Fourth Amendment as a wedge for imposing those terms, and to avoid questions of any kind."[24] In Blackmun's vision, Mrs. James apparently lacked the appropriate demeanor of gratitude for the public charity she received. His statements about her suggest that he did not see her as an unfortunate victim of poverty struggling to preserve some sense of dignity, but as an undeserving and ungrateful recipient of largesse.

The *Wyman* opinion is imbued with the assumption of the inherent moral weakness of the AFDC parent. Home visits are essential to assure the moral, religious, mental, and physical health of the children. The state is free to use the awesome power of the means of subsistence as a club to demand compliance. As for Mrs. James and other AFDC parents, who must either submit to the indignity of unannounced home visits or forego the benefits necessary to feed and clothe their children, he says that "[t]he choice is hers, and nothing of constitutional magnitude is involved."[25]

Jefferson v. Hackney

Texas had a problem in the early 1970s. The state constitution imposed a fixed dollar amount as the maximum that the state could spend on welfare, and this fixed amount became insufficient to meet the acknowledged need of the state's welfare recipients.[26] Texas solved the problem by reducing the level of benefits paid to needy people, but the state treated the various categories of public assistance differently. Texas chose to give the aged 100 percent of their need, the blind and disabled 95 percent, and AFDC recipients 50 percent of need (subsequently raised to 75 percent after AFDC families brought suit). The AFDC recipients argued that the scheme was unconstitutional because it lacked any rational basis for the especially harsh treatment of AFDC families. They argued that the actual motivation for the strikingly dissimilar treatment of the needy in Texas was racism. During the relevant time periods, blacks and Hispanics constituted 85 to 90 percent of the AFDC recipients, while in the other public assistance programs white Anglos were the dominant beneficiary group.

In *Jefferson v. Hackney*, Justice Rehnquist, writing for the majority, dismissed the racial discrimination argument, concluding that the AFDC recipients had nothing more than a "naked statistical argument" on the issue of racial discrimination. Rehnquist argued that Texas officials might rationally have concluded that "the aged and infirm are the least able of the categorical grant recipients to bear the hardships of an inadequate standard of living . . . that the young are more adaptable than the sick and elderly."[27] This might seem sensible, but why?

The Texas scheme left AFDC recipients in a position where they were receiving substantially less than they needed to maintain a marginal subsistence. There was no reason to believe that the suffering that accompanies inadequate food and shelter could be more easily borne by these families than by the aged and disabled. The rationality of the distinction between AFDC families and other recipients of public assistance depended on the superior ability of the AFDC family to "adapt." Because the family's need was fixed, the only possible adaptation to this desperate circumstance was to increase the family income, presumably through work. Thus Rehnquist's argument is implicitly premised on the assumption that jobs are available for the AFDC poor of Texas, and that we need only provide an incentive in the form of public benefits below their subsistence needs and they will take those jobs. Only in this sense are AFDC families better able to adjust than are the aged and disabled. Thus the background assumption in the Court's rationality analysis of Texas's law is that, notwithstanding the existence of employment opportunities, the AFDC poor had chosen to feed at the public trough rather than go earn their living.

Like Stewart's opinion in *Dandridge*, Rehnquist's opinion in *Jefferson* failed to explicitly label the poor as morally weak or degenerate. Yet the rhetoric of each opinion drew its power from that implicit premise. Just as Stewart's assertion of the need for an "equitable balance between welfare families and wage earner families" depended on an assumption of relative worthiness and desert between those two sets of families, Rehnquist's construction of the rationality of the Texas scheme depended on the assumption that able-bodied poor people were shirking work.

Rehnquist concluded his *Jefferson* opinion by "re-emphasiz[ing] what the court said in *Dandridge* . . . [T]he intractable economic, social, and even philosophical problems presented by public welfare assistance programs are not the business of the Court." Rehnquist thus left no doubt that the Court was not in the business of assuring wisdom, justice, and humanity in the administration of public assistance.

Bowen v. Gilliard

In *Bowen v. Gilliard*, AFDC recipients challenged the constitutionality of a provision of the 1984 Deficit Reduction Act that required the inclusion of all income of parents and siblings residing in the same house in the calculation of AFDC benefits for the family.[28] This apparently sensible provision posed a special problem for families with a child receiving child support payments from a nonresident parent. Prior to the 1984 act, AFDC families could have chosen to seek AFDC benefits only for the other children in the family and thus could have excluded any such child's support payments from the calculation of the family's income. This permitted the support-paying parent to financially support the child rather than have the child be a welfare recipient. The new law took away that option. Because the child's support payments were counted as family income, the custodial parent had no practical choice but to include the child in the AFDC application. Moreover, once such a child was included within the filing unit, the law required the assignment of that child's support payments to the state.

The AFDC families argued that the law put the family and child to a terrible choice. The family could send the child receiving support to another household. Or the family could accept the alteration in the relation between the child and the parent paying support by requiring the child to become a recipient of AFDC and making the state, and not the child, the beneficiary of the parent's support obligation. The AFDC family's plight was well expressed by Justice Brennan:

The Government has told a child who lives with a mother receiving public assistance that it cannot both live with its mother and be supported by its father. The child must either leave the care and custody of the mother, or forego the support of the father and become a Government client. The child is put to this choice not because it seeks Government benefits for itself, but because of a fact over which it has no control: the need of *other* household members for public assistance. A child who lives with one parent has, under the best of circumstances, a difficult time sustaining a relationship with both its parents. A crucial bond between a child and its parent outside the home, usually the father, is the father's commitment to care for the material needs of the child, and the expectation of the child that it may look to its father for such care. The Government has thus decreed that a condition of welfare eligibility for a mother is that her child surrender a vital connection with either the father or the mother.[29]

Notwithstanding the various constitutionally based challenges to this law, the majority of the Court, through an opinion authored by Justice Stevens, upheld the law. The opinion's rhetoric is primarily a combination of the helplessness plea and the familiar idea that because people have no lawful claim to welfare, the government is free to structure and condition the welfare scheme in more or less any fashion it chooses.

Stevens spoke of the tragedy he was helpless to avert:

> [A] number of needy families have suffered, and will suffer, as a result of the implementation of the DEFRA amendments to the AFDC program. Such suffering is frequently the tragic by-product of a decision to reduce or to modify benefits to a class of needy recipients. Under our structure of government, however, it is the function of Congress — not the courts — to determine whether the savings realized, and presumably used for other critical governmental functions, are significant enough to justify the costs to the individuals affected by such reductions.[30]

Yet again the justices chose their helplessness, and, as is typically the case, everyone knew that the governmental body Stevens charged with the power to avert the tragedy, Congress, was not going to do so.

Stevens concluded his opinion with the nearly ritualistic practice of quoting the *Dandridge* litany of intractable problems, a disempowered court, and a myriad of needy poor.

Schweiker v. Chilicky

Although the AFDC cases are the richest source of the rhetoric of poverty, cases involving other public assistance programs embody their own versions of this rhetoric. In these cases, the justices have conjured the specter of fraud and professed their helplessness to remedy the tragedies they saw before them.

In 1980 Congress passed legislation that set in motion an especially shameful episode in the history of public assistance. The law directed state agencies to review the eligibility of Social Security disability beneficiaries periodically and if the initial evaluation was adverse to the disabled worker, benefits were to be terminated.

Pursuant to this law, during the early 1980s, the government terminated the benefits of hundreds of thousands of workers. Although almost half of all initial evaluations resulted in termination of benefits, almost two-thirds of all appeals resulted in reinstatement. In a three-year period in the mid-1980s, by the government's own calculations, it wrongfully terminated and later reinstated approximately 200,000 workers. All of those workers were left without benefits for many months during a lengthy appeal process.

In *Schweiker v. Chilicky*, disabled workers whose benefits had been wrongfully terminated during this period sued and sought money damages from the state and federal officials responsible for cutting off their benefits, alleging that the defendants had violated their constitutional rights.[31] The majority of the Court concluded that the disabled workers were without any remedy against the government officials. Justice O'Connor, writing for the majority, concluded that only Congress could redress the workers' grievances. Her summary of the case is a perfect expression of judicial helplessness:

> In the end, respondents' various arguments are rooted in their insistent and vigorous contention that they simply have not been adequately recompensed for their injuries. . . . We agree that suffering months of delay in receiving the income on which one has depended for the very necessities of life cannot be fully remedied by the "belated restoration of back benefits." The trauma to respondents, and thousands of others like them, must surely have gone beyond what anyone of normal sensibilities would wish to see imposed on innocent disabled citizens. Nor would we care to "trivialize" the nature of the wrongs alleged in this case. Congress, however, has addressed the problems created by state agencies' wrongful termination of disability benefits. Whether or not we believe that its response was the best response, Congress is the body charged with making the inevitable compromises required in the design of a massive and complex welfare benefits program. Congress has discharged that responsibility to the extent that it affects the case before us, and we see no legal basis that would allow us to revise its decision.[32]

Thus *Schweiker* became another case in which the Court professed its helplessness to remedy an aspect of public assistance acknowledged to be tragic and cruel.

Lyng v. Castillo

The central rhetorical theme of the Court's cases dealing with the food stamp program has been the assumption that poor people will cheat. This assumption was on display in the 1986 case *Lyng v. Castillo*. The food stamp program provided lower food stamp benefits per person for larger households than for smaller ones because of the economies of scale in food purchase and preparation involved. Yet people living in the same house but purchasing food and preparing meals separately were treated as separate, distinct "households" for purposes of food stamp benefits. In the early 1980s Congress concluded that people were falsely claiming separate household status for the purpose of increasing their food stamp benefits. Congress addressed the perceived problem of fraud by amending the definition of "household" to include parents, children, and siblings who lived under the same roof, even if they did not purchase food and prepare meals as one household. Thus related persons were simply denied the ability to claim separate household status, while unrelated or more distantly related persons could still claim that status.

Food stamp families challenged the provision on constitutional grounds. As with other poverty laws, the law on its face seemed coherent. But the families argued that because Congress continued to recognize that truly separate households existed and that such households sensibly required more assistance, the denial of such status to their households was not rational.

Justice Marshall, in dissent, described the law's effect:

> [S]ome separate families live in the same house but cannot prepare meals together because of different work schedules. . . . Others may lack sufficient plates and utensils to accommodate more than a few persons at once, or may have only one burner on their stove. These extended families simply lack the option of cooking and eating together. For them, the legislative presumption in this case does far greater damage than merely prescribing with whom they must dine. By assuming that they realize economies of scale that they in fact cannot achieve, the regulation threatens their lives and health by denying them the minimal benefits provided to all other families of similar income and needs.[33]

In Marshall's view, to prevent some poor people from receiving more than their entitlement, the new law denied others what they needed.

Justice Stevens, writing for the majority, characterized the statute as a rough, but not irrational, response to the specter of poor people lying about their living arrangements to obtain federal benefits to which they were not entitled. This opinion was necessarily premised on the assumption that large numbers of people claim food stamp benefits beyond their lawful entitlement and that they will continue to do so to such a degree that a bluntly crafted, irrebuttable exclusion from benefits is a rational response.

Again, one way to see the premise of moral weakness in the rhetoric of poverty is to contrast the basic structure and assumptions of the welfare system with those of the federal tax system. The welfare system transfers wealth from taxpayers to poor people. The tax system also transfers wealth. Although we usually think of a tax as a wealth-taking rather than a transfer of wealth, when Congress crafts the structure of our system of tax liability, it in effect makes some people wealthier than others. This view of the tax system makes it akin to the welfare system — a government choice to transfer wealth, to make some people more or less wealthy. Yet the ways in which we implement the two systems are radically different. The tax system depends on self-assessment and reporting; audits are a rarity. In contrast, Congress assumes that the welfare system must be implemented and closely monitored based on the assumption of substantial fraud. The difference might be understood as an assumption that "most of us don't cheat, but most of them do." We hold onto that assumption even though it must surely be the case that the theft from the U.S. Treasury arising from unreported lawful and unlawful income each year dwarfs the entire welfare budget.

The Court's rhetoric in the contemporary jurisprudence of poverty meshes with certain cultural narratives. When, for example,

Justice Blackmun hints at child abuse by an AFDC mother in *Wyman*, and the reader provides some version of an assumption of the moral weakness of poor people, the text and the reader together create a whole and potentially powerful argument. When Justice Stewart in *Dandridge* speaks of the "intractable" problems and a "myriad" of potential recipients, readers may nod their heads, recognizing the familiar idea of our essential helplessness in the face of poverty. In the food stamp cases, where an essential premise is that a propensity exists among poor people to defraud, the Court's failure explicitly to state this premise may not be noticed at all if at some level we accept the culturally taught idea of the moral weakness of "the poor."

The Power of Rhetoric: Assumptions and Choices

The contemporary Court, in a range of cases dealing with the rights and interests of poor people, has adopted a non-interventionist approach. Essentially, the Court has left the matter of the law's treatment of people in poverty to the political processes. The justices have created texts abundant with the explicit, but mostly invited, assumption of the difference and moral weakness of those in poverty. And repeatedly they have stressed their helplessness in the matter.

This story of choice and rhetoric in the poverty cases provides a structure for thinking about the power of rhetoric and the responsibility of the citizen. Out of an understanding of the nature of the rhetoric of poverty — in judicial argument or political discourse — emerges a responsibility. Once we have informed ourselves we have no morally neutral position available. We must respond. Even silence is a morally charged position.

The essential points of this part of the chapter have relevance beyond the bounds of the poverty cases. Each case we read, whatever its subject, represents a choice imposed on other people backed by the threat or actuality of violence. It may be a choice to terminate a mother's relationship with her son, to send a man to death or a cage for the rest of his life, or to allow the carnage of an undeclared war to continue. Thus we have a responsibility to see the subject of our inquiry as clearly and fully as possible.

By its very nature, rhetoric does three things. It reveals, it obscures, and it invites. By what it asserts, rhetoric reveals various pieces of its subject. By what it fails to say, it obscures other important pieces of its subject. And, perhaps most powerfully, by suggestion and indirect reference, it invites us to bring certain presuppositions about the subject to the reading.

The Court's rhetoric of poverty has conceptually segregated the poor in various ways. When Justice Stewart in *Dandridge* demanded an "equitable balance" between welfare families and families with an employed person, he conceptually separated families receiving public assistance from other families. Justice Rehnquist in *Jefferson* validated the Texas AFDC scheme by separating AFDC recipients into the undeserving able-bodied poor, and the deserving infirm and aged poor. Running through the disability benefits and food stamps cases is the specter of fraud, which in turn depends on the separation of recipients of public assistance as a group especially likely to defraud the government.

The very act of conceptual segregation has rhetorical power. When those segregated are defined by their difference from the dominant class, the act of segregation suggests not simply difference but also deviance. The norm is inherently defined by the dominant group; the segregated group is defined by deviance from that norm.

The segregation of the poor and the assertion of their moral deviance are intertwined. Accepting the us / them construct makes the assertion of moral deviance easier to accept, and, reciprocally, the acceptance of the idea of their moral deviance reinforces the idea of difference. While few people think of themselves as so prone to child abuse that unannounced home visits by government agents are appropriate in the absence of probable cause, we can think of "others" in that way. Thus the two rhetorical themes work together, iterating and reiterating the essential message.

In its assertion or suggestion of the difference and deviance of the poor, the rhetoric of poverty reveals and obscures various parts of its subject. It reveals the reality of criminal and immoral behavior among the poor; the rich are not the only ones who defraud the government and abuse their children. At the same time, it obscures the aspects of poverty that reflect our own lives. All Americans, poor or not, struggle to find and hold jobs, to raise children, and to resist the temptation to cheat. We all possess dreams and aspirations. Sometimes we succeed, often we fail.

The arguments of the Court's opinions in the poverty cases are much more than rhetorical forms. They are a lens through which we see poverty. Once we accept certain assumptions, we are done, the answer to the legal issue is a foregone conclusion. For example, if we see the AFDC parent as different, prone to child abuse, and an ungrateful recipient of public largesse, the legal issue of whether the government can demand home visits to protect the welfare of the child as a condition of the largesse seems easily answered. By contrast, if we see that person as akin to us, as someone struggling to hold a family together and keep a sense of personal dignity through it all, the legal issue becomes more problematic.

The rhetoric of poverty invites us to provide a part of the picture, to bring to the debate the culturally taught, stereotypical assumptions about the poor. This invitation is the most powerful aspect of the rhetoric. In the *Wyman* case, Justice Blackmun never said that Mrs. James physically abused her son; he instead told the story of the "infant Maurice." He did not say that AFDC mothers were different; he merely spoke of the public interest in protecting children from "exploitation." But in doing so, Blackmun invited us to see a picture that the narratives of our cultural teachings have predisposed most of us to see.

If, instead, Blackmun had stated explicitly that AFDC mothers were different and prone to child abuse, his arguments might have had less influence; some would probably have mixed feelings about the accuracy of these charges. It is precisely because Blackmun invites but does not speak such blunt assumptions that we are likely to nod our heads at the sense of it all, filling out the meaning of the text by providing some version of the cultural stereotypes that make Blackmun's argument coherent, if not compelling.

The assumptions and experiences of the individual, the purpose and context of the argument, and other variables will affect the nature of any actual and particular reading of these opinions. Still, for all readers drawn from a culture that teaches the difference and deviance of the poor, the assertion or suggestion of those cultural themes is not simply and easily sloughed off.

The rhetoric of poverty also works in a more general way to influence our sense of those in poverty. The experience of reading this rhetoric may diminish the possibility for empathy. So long as we think of those in poverty as "them" and not like "us," we are less likely to share in their sense of pain and humiliation. We can imagine that they do not suffer as we would, or that their suffering, unlike ours, is inevitable or even deserved. As Richard Rorty, an important contemporary philosopher and social critic, has told us, "[Human solidarity] is to be achieved not by inquiry but by imagination, the imaginative ability to see strange people as fellow sufferers. Solidarity is not discovered by reflection but created. It is created by increasing our sensitivity to the particular details of the pain and humiliation of other, unfamiliar sorts of people."[34]

Our inability to imagine the poor as strong, successful, and responsible people who win the battles of life also blocks empathy. The persistent idea of the "passive poor" in "the underclass" keeps blocking our imagination. Yet the story of people in poverty in this country has often been a story of strength and success. Against all odds, facing social stigma, working through maddening systems of public assistance, many poor women and men have kept their families together and maintained safe and decent lives in the midst of conditions that would seem to make family disintegration inescapable.[35] Many fail, but many succeed. The rhetoric of poverty highlights only the stories of failure and obscures the stories of success.

The contemporary Court's rhetoric of helplessness essentially seeks to move the reader to a position beyond choice. Within this rhetoric, the problem of poverty is either a matter of personal transformation for which we cannot be responsible or a matter of such daunting complexity that we cannot solve it. The judicial helplessness version of the argument is expressed in the oft repeated litany from *Dandridge*: the problem of poverty is "not the business of the Court."[36]

This profession of helplessness in each of its various manifestations, like all pieces of rhetoric, reveals and obscures parts of its subject. The "personal transformation" argument for our helplessness highlights the real problem of individual responsibility in the matter of poverty; some people remain poor in part because they lack the will to change. The "too many forces" argument highlights the real power of history and tradition; when generations of Americans have grown up with poverty as an enduring feature of the cultural landscape, the assumption that poverty is built into our society becomes hard to slough off.

In the process of highlighting these features of poverty, the helplessness argument obscures another view, one well expressed by Michael Katz:

> When Americans talk about poverty, some things remain unsaid.
> Mainstream discourse about poverty, whether liberal or conservative,

largely stays silent about politics, power, and equality. But poverty, after all, is about distribution; it results because some people receive a great deal less than others. Descriptions of the demography, behavior, or beliefs of subpopulations cannot explain the patterned inequalities evident in every era of American history. These result from styles of dominance, the way power is exercised, and the politics of distribution.

Poverty no longer is natural; it is a social product. As nations emerge from the tyranny of subsistence, gain control over the production of wealth, develop the ability to feed their citizens and generate surpluses, poverty becomes not the product of scarcity, but of political economy. Yet with few exceptions (such as some of the discussions during the Great Depression of the 1930s or the internal colonialism debate of the 1960s), this is not the way Americans have talked and written about poverty.[37]

The judicial helplessness argument, however, does not rely on the assumption that the problem of poverty is intractable. Although the assertion of the complexity and intractability of poverty is typically woven into the Court's rhetoric, the plea of judicial helplessness requires only the assertion that the Court is not the proper institution to act.

The plea of judicial helplessness is an especially strong rhetorical move because it sweeps off the table the issue of the wisdom or justice of the outcome of the Court's ruling. It diverts the reader's eye to the abstract and obscure issue of the separation of powers and the appropriate role for the judicial institution. As it highlights these real but abstract issues, it obscures the inescapable element of choice in the judge's articulation of his own jurisdictional boundaries.[38] The plea of judicial helplessness directs the debate to the bloodless ground of the separation of powers doctrine and hence away from the particular suffering of those who inhabit the Kafkaesque world of poverty.

The rhetoric of poverty thus works on the reader in many ways. It creates a framework for viewing the legal issues of poverty that is a product of what the rhetoric says, what it fails to say, and what it invites the reader to supply. The potential for influence arises not from the force of its syllogisms and string cites, but instead from the vision of poverty and law it creates and invites.

The Responsibility of the Reader

When we read a judicial opinion in a poverty case we are engaged in an activity with moral connotation. When you read, for example, the *Wyman* case, and you remain silent, you have chosen not to speak, not to act as critic, not to engage in explicit normative discourse. You make this choice after reading a case that says that a mother receiving AFDC benefits must either allow the government access to her home without probable cause, warrant, or notice, or the mother must go without the benefits that are essential to feed and care for herself and her child. What reaction to this case is without moral connotation?

The very act of reading the Supreme Court's poverty cases imposes a responsibility on the reader, one which pertains to our citizenship whether or not we are members of the legal profession. We know this responsibility in its other manifestations. If we were members of a church community and read a text from the governing body setting forth the church's position on the ordination of women, we would not imagine that we could read and be silent without moral connotation. If our city council passed a resolution regarding the rights of gay men and women in the community, we would not suppose that we could read that document and have no responsibility whatsoever for its message. It is the responsibility of a reader within a community to choose a position on the texts that express that community's position on matters that really count.

What, then, is the ethic of the reader? It is to read with the largest measure of care, imagination, and knowledge we can muster. We should do more than simply embrace the arguments of the text. Breaking past the confines of the formal arguments, we must use our imagination and our knowledge of the world to discern how these legal choices will be played out. We must become the most skillful readers we can be, because the process of reading is always followed by the necessity of our own choice in the matter, the choice to speak or be silent.

A description of poetic metaphor provides a way of thinking about how our responsibility as readers of rhetorical argument might be discharged. Max Black, a poetry scholar, has described the process whereby a poetic metaphor provides meaning.[39] He asks that you imagine looking at the starry night sky through a piece of painted glass on which several lines have been etched. You would see a night sky with some stars revealed and others obscured. Black suggests that experiencing a poetic metaphor is somehow like looking through the etched glass — the metaphor reveals and obscures various parts of its subject, creating a new vision.

Borrowing Black's allegory, we might say that the Court's rhetoric is our etched glass and the night sky is the context and legal issues presented in the case at hand. Thus the reader's responsibility is to look past the vision composed by the etched glass and see the context and legal issues as completely as possible.

The essential flaw of this allegory as a description of either reading poems or reading judicial opinions is in its suggestion that the subject, the night sky, is a fixed thing, external to the observer / reader. When we encounter a poetic metaphor, our own sense of its subject — whether it is an abstraction like love or a tangible thing like a tree — becomes part of the reading and part of the meaning.[40]

We face a similar problem in the "reading" of all argument. We bring to any reading some sense of its subject. Rhetoric seeks to reveal and obscure, but it invites too. We will be invited to supply our own sense of the subject. It is as though we are looking through an etched glass at a night sky that we in part create in the process of looking. Thus we must struggle to bring our own assumptions out of the murky place of the unstated and assumed, into the light of explicit assertion, where we can judge their truth for ourselves.

The question posed by this chapter is where shall we choose to stand on the rhetorical field. We, as a society, seem prepared to abolish the legal entitlement to public assistance, to bring forth "the end of welfare as we know it." At this time especially, as readers and as citizens, we have an ethical obligation to ponder and choose our perspective. The Court's rhetoric of poverty has carved out a viewing point on the legal issues of poverty. It is a relatively comfortable niche — either a place beyond choice or a seat of judgment from which we see the poor and judge their moral strength, winnowing out the undeserving from the deserving.

There are other viewing points we might choose. We might acknowledge the inherent element of choice for all of us in these matters and the responsibility that comes with that acknowledgment. We might struggle to see and empathize with the suffering of the poor. We might question our own moral strength. From these other, less comfortable viewing points, we might still see the Court's choices as right. But to do so we would have to accept the essential idea that this was an instance where suffering that might be alleviated ought not to be addressed, not because we were beyond choice in the matter, but rather because we made the hardest of choices — the choice that suffering we might relieve ought nonetheless to continue.

The rhetoric of poverty shelters us from our choices. We can imagine that the suffering of the poor is just or that we are helpless. But our history is replete with the most elegant of rhetorical facades built around the most horrific of legal choices. And we must wonder whether our choices about poverty will bring upon us and our children the tragedy and shame that historically has attended those who take the shelter of rhetoric in a storm of human suffering.

[95]

The Feminist Nomos

Men dominate and oppress women. The law facilitates this domination and oppression. Each effort at law reform on behalf of women essentially fails. Absent a radical transformation of the relations between men and women, none of this is going to change to any significant degree. This is what feminist legal scholarship tells us.

I hate this despairing message. That I believe it to be true only makes me hate it all the more.

There is, however, another message in feminist legal scholarship, one which does not deny the reality of domination and oppression but adds a vision of redemption. In this strain of the scholarship there is a bridge between the reality of today's world and a future in which being a woman does not make one a special object of domination, oppression, and physical violence. This redemptive vision does not depend on the illusion of an imminent and dramatic transformation of the world. Like all true redemptive visions, it offers instead a way of living and working within one's unredeemed reality.

As Robert Cover states in "Nomos and Narrative," we inhabit a normative universe — a nomos — within which "[w]e constantly create and maintain a world of right and wrong, of lawful and unlawful, of valid and void."[1] Feminist legal scholars are engaged in the activity of building and maintaining a feminist nomos. The law they create diverges from the state's law. The world they imagine is radically different from our world. Their messages of despair and redemption manifest the tension between today's world and the one they imagine.

The law that governs the lives of women, like all law, is a product of both interpretation and commitment. Interpretation truly becomes law only when someone is prepared to act upon it. Commitment and the corresponding actions of the state's actors — judges, juries, prosecutors, police officers, and others — transform meaning into law. For instance, the justices of the Supreme Court must not only be prepared to say whether the Constitution asures women personal choice in their reproductive lives, they must also invoke the state's apparatus of force to assure or deny the choices of women. The police officer at the barricades in front of the abortion clinic must not only possess an interpretive understanding of what the laws governing this civil disturbance say, that officer must also act on that interpretation by wielding the apparatus of force and violence. The state's law emerges from the combination of interpretation and a commitment to act on that interpretation.

But the state's actors have no monopoly on commitment. The individuals who seek to block access to abortion clinics, as well as those who come to protect the clinic and the women who seek abortions there, also possess an interpretive understanding and a commitment to that understanding. When an individual is committed to a law opposed to the state's law, that commitment may manifest itself in dramatic examples of civil disobedience. As the violence of the state was brought to bear upon the bodies of the civil rights marchers in America in the 1960s, the country was left with an indelible and shameful image of the racism of the state and with an equally indelible but inspirational image of civil disobedience. The society was also witnessing the creation of law when the state, committed to its interpretive understandings, clashed with individuals no less (and in the end even more) committed to another understanding.

Feminist legal scholars are engaged in the struggle to create a new framework of meaning within the law and have demonstrated a commitment to that meaning. Their disagreement with the state is a disagreement of the most destabilizing sort. Unlike scholars who take the state to task for particular errors in its rules but who otherwise accept the basic premises of the state's law, feminist legal scholars deny the most basic assumptions of the state's law. While traditional legal scholarship says, "You've made a mistake here," feminist scholarship says to the state, "You've wholly misconceived the world in which we live." By advancing this radically destabilizing message, these scholars have put themselves into the struggle to remake legal meaning. They are engaged in the maintenance of a feminist nomos that stands in opposition to the state. And by this activity they demonstrate a commitment that is different from the engagement of the traditional legal scholar.

Feminist scholars teach that the law that shall govern the lives of women will be a product of a web of interpretive commitments. The state's commitment to its law is a part, but only a part, of the web. The work of these scholars reminds us that we face inescapable questions — to what law are we committed and what is the nature and strength of that commitment? Our choices are none but those. There is no quiet, safe, easily occupied vantage point from which we might imagine that we are removed from the battleground of the creation of law which shall signal either renewed oppression or new respect for women. By our individual acts, speech, and most commonly by silence, we each participate in the creation and maintenance of the law.

Feminist Legal Scholarship

Feminist legal scholars have revealed the various ways in which the rule of law has been the rule of men, a systematic domination and oppression of women.[2] They have described the experience of women as victims of rape who are themselves put on trial, as victims of sexual harassment to whom the law offers little meaningful shelter, as battered women who when driven to self-defense find themselves unable to express their circumstances in the vocabulary of the law, as workers who are "protected" from gainful employment, and as persons who have only a limited say in what happens to their own bodies.

Feminists have also crafted their own methods of scholarship. Rejecting the primarily abstract and tautological style that characterizes much traditional legal scholarship, they have emphasized context over abstraction, pragmatic solutions over devotion to general rules. But their most significant distinguishing trait is their insistence on the narrative form of expression. Feminist legal scholars tell stories of battered women, raped women, women humiliated in the workplace, and other stories of oppression. Although this emphasis on narrative is not unique to their work (for example, as we have discussed previously, much of the most important legal scholarship on race has for some time relied on an acknowledgment of the power of narrative), feminist legal scholars have been insistent and straightforward proponents of a distinctive mix of pragmatism and storytelling.

Most traditional legal scholarship seeks to justify existing law or argues for reform. Some feminist legal scholars see neither a justification for the laws they study nor the possibility of meaningful reform of those laws. They have shown how ostensible reform in legal doctrines, including those relating to rape and sexual harassment, has produced little meaningful change in legal outcomes for women. They have told us that our law is depraved, that our traditional scholarship is misconstructed, and that the very enterprise of law reform is problematic, if not pointless. It is a stunningly powerful and destabilizing set of accusations.

The terms "feminist legal scholarship" and "feminist legal scholars," like all such phrases, are reductive and potentially misleading. They sweep together writers of differing political ideology, those who disagree about the desired sort of law reform with those who disagree on the very usefulness of reform per se. For example, my summary of the despairing message of feminist legal scholarship outlined above is a composite of the work of various scholars, and not all feminist legal scholars would agree that this is their message.

Such a categorization also obscures important differences in experience, perspective, and focus — differences that derive from race, economic class, sexual orientation, and other factors.[3] Indeed, Ruth Colker, Kimberle Crenshaw, Mari Matsuda, and Patricia Williams have argued eloquently against the "essentialism" that sometimes characterizes feminist legal thought. There are many bases by which people deem others different and less worthy. In talking about one particular basis for discrimination, we can lose sight of others. Moreover, differently constructed bases for discrimination against women suggest different agendas for reform, so that a choice to focus on one perspective alone may in fact yield an agenda that does little or nothing for other, differently situated women. Still, one must use categories and labels to talk sensibly about anything. The challenge is to bear in mind the particular and contingent quality of our focus.

There is a group of scholars whose work reveals sufficient commonality that the phrase "feminist legal scholarship" is in order. These writers share a set of basic assumptions and tools which are described by Katharine Bartlett in her article "Feminist Legal

Methods."[4] Bartlett identified three methods that define feminist legal scholarship.

First, feminist legal scholars "ask the woman question"; they seek to identify the ways in which legal rules, typically gender-neutral on their face, disadvantage and oppress women. Second, they engage in what Bartlett calls "feminist practical reasoning," a pragmatic mode of reasoning. Third, feminist legal scholars tell stories of oppression as a "consciousness-raising" activity.

Asking the woman question is a method that cuts across doctrinal areas, from rape to contract law. Bartlett described the method in the following terms:

> Once adopted as a method, asking the woman question is a method of critique as integral to legal analysis as determining the precedential value of a case, stating the facts, or applying law to facts. "Doing law" as a feminist means looking beneath the surface of law to identify the gender implications of rules and assumptions underlying them and insisting upon applications of rules that do not perpetuate women's subordination. It means recognizing that the woman question always has potential relevance.[5]

As with all methods, asking the woman question carries ideological baggage. To make this question the central activity of one's work makes sense only if one assumes, as legal feminists do, that gender oppression is a real and powerful force and that much of our law reflects and facilitates that oppression.

The second defining method feminist legal scholars employ, feminist legal practical reasoning, is a search for "pragmatic responses to concrete dilemmas" as opposed to an intellectual manipulation of abstract precepts.[6] Although all reasoning invokes both context and abstractions, feminist reasoning emphasizes context. This attention to context has produced a parallel preference for legal rules of a less specific and thus less constraining nature. Bartlett observes, "[Feminist legal scholars] have argued that individualized factfinding is often superior to the application of bright-line rules, and that reasoning from context allows a greater respect for difference and for the perspectives of the powerless."[7]

The focus on context over abstraction and the taste for less specific rules is not unique to feminist legal reasoning. Versions of these ideas can be found in a range of movements, from legal realism through critical legal studies to the recent rediscovery of pragmatism by legal scholars. Still, the use of practical reasoning combined with asking the woman question has produced a distinctive mode of reasoning which, in one form or another, permeates the scholarship of the feminists.

The last, and most controversial, of the feminist methods is the use of narrative for what Bartlett, Leslie Bender, and others call consciousness-raising.

> Feminist consciousness-raising creates knowledge by exploring common experiences and patterns that emerge from shared tellings of life events. What were experienced as personal hurts individually suffered reveal themselves as a collective experience of oppression.[8]

The work of these writers is replete with stories about the authors' experiences, the experiences of other particular women, and stories about women's lives told in a general way.

Thus feminist legal scholars start with a knowledge of the oppression of women and the assumption that the law reflects and facilitates that oppression. In their analysis of the law, they focus on context, seeking to bring into the field of relevance considerations that traditional scholarship has shut out. By telling their narratives, they seek to raise the consciousness of their readers and perhaps to help heal the wounds of those who suffer.

This body of work has achieved recognized status within the academic community. There are symposia on various gender issues and on feminist legal scholarship itself. Most law school curricula today have at least one course directed to gender issues, in which the readings include exposure to feminist legal scholarship. Law schools invite feminist scholars to deliver lectures as part of lecture series with impressive names that actually pay money for the talks.

Critical responses to feminist legal scholarship take various standard forms. Some resist, or reject, the basic premise. Echoing a common reaction to arguments about racism, some critics accuse the feminist writers of overstating the phenomenon of oppression. To the extent these critics acknowledge gender oppression, it is seen as a piece of history rather than a description of today's world. Women in the late twentieth century, in this critique, are not oppressed and certainly not oppressed by law. In this view, whatever sexism remains is aberrational and not a source of real constraint for women today.

There is, however, another, more damning characterization of feminist legal scholarship. Critics may challenge its very status as real scholarship. The feminist method of asking the woman question can trigger the charge that the result is political tract rather than serious study. Similarly, the use of narrative can be described as undisciplined storytelling, not real analysis. This second kind of criticism seeks to exclude this scholarship from the realm of writings that are worth taking seriously, and it is powerful because it dismisses, rather than engages, its subject.

Other critics accept the reality of oppression that the narratives depict, yet find no plan for action within the scholarship. Law reform seems futile so long as the basic and ingrained sense of women as less worthy pervades the culture. And changing those basic assumptions seems wholly daunting. Beyond its message of oppression, these readers find no point to the work.

These standard criticisms depend upon a commonly held conception of legal scholarship as nothing more than academic work designed to analyze the law and, finding the law wanting, to promote its reform. When they apply this conception of legal scholarship to feminist work, they see feminist scholarship as just another form of the game played by scholars of the various academic camps. While it is true that feminist legal scholars do play the game (and often play it very well), they also do something else — they participate in the maintenance of a normative community whose law is opposed to the state's law. This understanding of their work complicates the process of critical appraisal.

Community and Conflict

This perspective on feminist legal scholarship derives from the work of Robert Cover, and from this understanding emerges a different sense of the nature and purposes of that scholarship, as well as a sharper sense of its redemptive qualities.

In his extraordinary paper "Nomos and Narrative," Cover created an original and compelling vision of law.[9] The centerpiece of his paper is the concept of the *nomos*, the normative universe. The lessons he taught, although of the widest possible relevance, illuminate in a special way both feminist legal scholarship and the law to which it reacts. Through Cover's vision, one can see feminist legal scholarship as part of the process of creating law and maintaining a normative community.

Cover taught that we live in a normative universe that is composed only in part of the rules and institutions that we commonly identify as our legal structure. Our nomos is also composed of the stories we tell:

> No set of legal institutions or prescriptions exists apart from the narratives that locate it and give it meaning. For every constitution there is an epic, for each decalogue a scripture. Once understood in the context of the narratives that give it meaning, law becomes not merely a system of rules to be observed, but a world in which we live.[10]

Our legal rules and the stories we tell that provide the essential context for those rules are inseparable. In Cover's words, "Every prescription is insistent in its demand to be located in discourse — to be supplied with history and destiny, beginning and end, explanation and purpose. And every narrative is insistent in its demand for its prescriptive point, its moral."[11]

This confluence of rule and narrative may be sufficient to yield a particular kind of meaning. For example, one might sensibly answer the hypothetical question of whether a woman's choice to terminate a pregnancy is or is not protected by the Constitution by resort to the language of the constitutional text and our particular narratives about those texts and about the circumstances of women and the nature of abortion.

But this sort of activity is only a part of the construction of the constitutional law relating to abortion. The construction of the law of abortion is also a product of commitment — the commitment of the state, certainly, to its law and the narratives it chooses, but also the commitment of individuals to their law, which may be opposed to the state's law. As Cover wrote, "The normative universe is held together by the force of interpretive commitments — some small and private, others immense and public. These commitments — of officials and of others — do determine what law means and what law shall be."[12] Judges must act on their interpretations, as must police officers, doctors, lawyers, women seeking abortions, and those who oppose abortion. This web of interpretive commitments determines the law of abortion.

The laws of abortion, rape, sexual harassment, and other important laws that govern the lives of women are each a product of precepts, narrative, and commitment in a world in which the state has no monopoly on legal interpretation or on commitment. Individuals can find their own meaning from precepts and narratives and can act on that meaning.

The state and the individual, however, are not equally situated in their lawmaking capacity. Only the state can summon the apparatus of force and violence that is the state's, yet the state's monopoly on violence is imperfect because the individual can also write his or her commitment in blood. When a community of committed individuals are prepared to live by their law in the face of the state's opposition, it may be the state that backs down.

Cover provided a powerful example of the significance of narrative and commitment in the construction of legal meaning in his recounting of the *Bob Jones University* case.[13] In this case the Court held that the I.R.S. had acted within its statutory authority in denying tax-exempt status to a school that discriminated on the basis of race, even though the school justified its racism on religious grounds. The Church of God in Christ, Mennonite, although not a party to the litigation and not an institution that shared the racist premises of the litigant, submitted a brief advancing the special significance of the First Amendment's guarantee of religious freedom. The Mennonite brief consisted of a narrative of the church's "tortuous history." The church's followers had been slaughtered by the thousands during the sixteenth century in Europe and had since that time consisted of migratory communities of "defenseless people looking for a place to be." For the Mennonites, the meaning of the First Amendment's "free exercise" text was a product of this narrative. In their brief, they wrote, "[Our church history] has left within us an extremely high regard for religious liberty. We consider the religious liberty that this nation concedes as possibly its greatest virtue."[14] The church's narratives combined with the First Amendment text yielded a particular and powerful interpretation of constitutional law.

The Mennonite example is also one of commitment. They are committed to the law of their normative community and are prepared to live by their commitment:

Our faith and understanding of scripture enjoin respect and obedience to the secular governments under which we live. We recognize them as institutions established by God for order in society. For that reason

[107]

alone, without the added distress of punitive action for failure to do so, we always exercise ourselves to be completely law-abiding. Our religious beliefs, however, are very deeply held. When these beliefs collide with the demands of society, our highest allegiance must be toward God, and we must say with men of God of the past, "We must obey God rather than men," and these are the crises from which we would be spared. [15]

This assertion is the statement of a normative community and not simply the argument of an advocate. The Mennonites are not merely seeking, like the advocate, a change in the state's law; they are also doing something much more powerful. They have created law and are asserting their commitment to that law in the context of a history in which the Mennonites' opposition to the state's law has demanded a real and high price.

Legal meaning always depends on precepts and narratives manifested by a web of interpretive commitments. This is equally true in the less dramatic instances of law's creation. Most people are lawbreakers, even though they do not think of themselves in those terms. As we've discussed earlier, individuals resist the state's law in a mix of important and less important contexts. In defiance of the state's law, we may drive faster than the speed limit, overstate our tax deductions, refuse combat service, defy police orders to disperse, trespass on private property, take illegal drugs, or seek to shut down abortion clinics. When we engage in these kinds of activities, we are relying on an oppositional law, a law that trumps the state's law. This oppositional law may be an understanding that cutting through a person's backyard to avoid walking around the block is not unlawful, or it may be the law of one's religious community that calls for the cessation of abortion and for personal action to achieve that end. Even when we acknowledge that we are just plain breaking the law because it serves our self-interest and we see little risk of de-tection, we are not acting without principle. In such instances, we likely suppose that the state's law is unworthy. Some version of a principle that makes our lawbreaking a sane and coherent way of behaving is likely always to be present. Most of us are lawbreakers, few of us are sociopaths. This ceaseless activity of action, sometimes in conformity with the state's law, often in accordance with another sense of law, is a product of living within a normative universe that is as much a part of our existence as the physical world we inhabit.

When a group of people share precepts and narratives and a sense of commitment to the realization of a redeemed world, they create law and constitute a normative community. Maintaining a normative community demands the teaching of shared precepts and narratives. This point is most obviously exemplified by — but not limited to — religious communities, in which schools, study classes, and religious leaders ceaselessly teach the precepts and narratives of their particular faith. The meaning that emerges from precept and narrative is the law for the members of that community. This law forms a bridge between the present reality and the vision of a world to come. In Cover's words, "Law may be viewed as a system of tension or a bridge linking a concept of reality to an imagined alternative."[16] This imagined alternative world is not simply a utopian vision. Each member of the community must have some commitment to acting upon the law they share. Without such a commitment, the person is not a participant in the creation of law and the maintenance of a normative community.

When the state's law and the law of the community clash, the commitments of the state and the community are each tested. When the state is truly committed to its law, the community may formally defer to the state's apparatus of power and violence. Sometimes the state gives way to the community's law. But at no time does the normative community understand "the law" to mean only the state's version of law, even as they sometimes yield to the state. Whether their commitment is written in the blood of the martyr or some lesser form, they create and possess their own law.

The Feminist Nomos

The methods feminist legal scholars use are different from the methods used by apologists for the state's law precisely because they cannot do their work by the same methods. It is not a matter of preference or feminine predisposition. Their methods reflect their essential purposes — the creation of law, the maintenance of a normative community, and the pursuit of redemption.

The basic precept of the legal feminist nomos is embodied in "asking the woman question." When feminists do so they are implicitly asserting the backdrop that gives the question its significance and sense: the reality of gender oppression, the role of law in the maintenance of that oppression, and the judgment that this condition is unjust. The more particular precepts that emerge from the feminist legal scholarship—the advancement of a particular piece of law reform such as the rape shield law—for example, all evolve from this basic set of assumptions.

Maintaining the feminist nomos also demands the pedagogical sharing of stories. These narratives combine with precepts to yield legal interpretation. For example, the precept that women should be free of sexual harassment in the workplace combines with narratives of the workplace to yield meaning. The mix of narrative and precept is what provides definition to the very term "sexual harassment." Thus the different stories that men and women have about the workplace yield different senses of what is and what is not harassment, and freight the rule with more or less significance. Sexual harassment is very serious business for the feminist because her stories are about her humiliation and violation. It is less serious for someone who possesses stories about "good-natured" give-and-take on the job or about women's repressed desire for dirty talk.

When feminist legal scholars tell stories, they are teaching legal meaning. By the same method, they are defining and maintaining a community. The stories that women share establish the interpersonal ties within the normative community. The knowledge that someone else has suffered in ways that are similar to one's own suffering is a powerful source for connection. The narratives form a roughly shared discourse by which other women are brought within the community. The stories are at once both moralizing discourse, teaching the listener something about the reality of oppression, and a source of bond and community for those who tell and hear them.

"Feminist practical reasoning" is also an inevitable part of the expression of the feminist vision of law. When the legal feminist rejects the dominant way of intellectualizing about law through a reliance on abstractions and syllogisms, and insists instead on telling stories, she is in effect rejecting the apologist's stories that are imbedded in the abstractions. The narratives that give coherence to the state's law are those that have been dominant within the culture. These are not the narratives of the feminist nomos. Thus the state's apologist can rely on an abstract line of reasoning that invites the reader to bring the culture's dominant images and assumptions to the debate. As discussed in previous chapters, the judge who seeks to justify the prohibition of affirmative action need not tell out loud the stories of blacks as persons who seek unearned and undeserved advantage; the judge who allows the perpetuation of a cruel system of public assistance need not be explicit to invoke the premise of the undeserving poor. Similarly, the scholar or judge who seeks to justify the exclusion of women from combat service need not state (or defend) a belief that women lack the blood lust necessary to be killers in the cause of patriotism.

The legal feminist thus tells stories aloud in part because she must overcome the other stories that are already powerfully present within the culture. Advertising, movies, and television typically foster stereotypes about women as different and less worthy than men, and beyond these fabricated depictions, most women's lives reflect the effects of these stories.

Legal feminists are not refusing to talk abstractions and syllogisms because they eschew tough-minded reasoning — they do not. But to get the initial premises right, they have to displace the culture's stories with their own. To advance their law, they must provide not just new precepts but also new narratives to fill those precepts with interpretive meaning.

Every normative community must have a sense of boundaries, a sense of exclusion and inclusion; there must be outsiders to have any meaningful sense of being an insider. Therefore a sense of the feminist nomos is also revealed in the internal debate about who can rightfully claim to be a feminist and who cannot. (A good example of this debate is the question of whether a man can be a feminist. Legal feminists are split on this question.) In this debate, the boundaries of the normative community are at stake.

The feminist nomos, like other normative communities, is racked with the tension between the world as it is and the other world that is to come. Those who experience this tension express the alternative responses of redemption or insularity.

Robert Cover described these two types of response in the context of the nineteenth-century abolitionist movement.[17] The radical Garrisonian abolitionists agreed with those who interpreted the Constitution to countenance slavery, and responded by a move to insularity. They turned away from the Constitution, refusing to accept it as the sacred text. As part of a philosophy of perfectionism, they eschewed the state and its law. In contrast, the abolitionists whom Cover calls the "redemptive constitutionalists" insisted on a constitutional law that repudiated slavery and the legal apparatus that propped up that horrific institution. This redemptive response was expressed in Frederick Douglass's conclusion "that the Constitution of the United States — inaugurated to 'form a more perfect union, establish justice, insure domestic tranquility, provide for the common defense, promote the general welfare, and secure the blessings of liberty' — could not well have been designed at the same time to maintain and perpetuate a system of rapine and murder like slavery."[18] Douglass and the other radical constitutionalists responded to the tension between the reality of slavery and the vision of a world without slavery by holding on to the redemptive possibilities posed by their constitutional law, however much the state's constitutional law remained opposed.

The legal feminist nomos has also displayed the tension between reality and vision. A powerful example can be found in the work of Catharine MacKinnon, one of the most prominent of the legal feminist scholars.[19] MacKinnon has devoted much of her work to law reform, particularly in the areas of sexual harassment and pornography, and her path-breaking work on sexual harassment contributed to the development of the federal law known as Title VII.[20] MacKinnon was also a primary draftsperson for a controversial Indianapolis antipornography ordinance. In this work, she expresses the redemptive possibility, devoting herself to building the bridge between reality and vision. Yet in other aspects of her work, she expresses what seems like an insular response, depicting heterosexual relations as inherently violent, demeaning, and subjugating to the woman; she seems to forsake the possibility of legal reform to call for radical social transformation as the only real hope for meaningful change. When a feminist is unable to hold to any form of redemptive response, she leaves the legal feminist nomos and enters another overlapping but distinct normative community composed of those who accept the essential teachings of the legal feminist community but who have given up on law as an instrument of reform. Catharine MacKinnon's work suggests that she lives at various times in each of these two communities.

Thus the tension within the legal feminist nomos is revealed in the sectarian splintering of the community. Legal feminists split on ideological grounds, with liberals espousing the possibilities for change within the existing structure and radicals doubting that law reform will accomplish much in the absence of radical social transformation.

The "essentialism debate" is perhaps the most vivid reflection of such faultlines within the community. Feminist legal scholarship often speaks of "women" as though they constituted a single homogeneous category, and the stories most often told make sense only in the context of a white, heterosexual woman not living in poverty. MacKinnon's work, for example, has spawned its own essentialism debate; other feminists have rejected her depiction of women as essentially victims of male sexual domination, noting especially the obvious alternative of lesbian relationships.

The sectarian splintering of the feminist community is not unique. Every normative community is inherently unstable as long as the very process that gives rise to its creation — the generation and teaching of new precepts and stories — continues. As soon as it becomes a community, some of its members will speak to challenge the dominant precepts and narratives. When the differences become large, sectarian splintering begins as a reflection of the tension between reality and vision. The legal feminists have not, and will not, bring forth the millennium, and in this real and oppressive world some feminists will seek their own way.

When feminist scholarship is measured by its converts and its connection to formal law reform, some will find it easy to dismiss the work as a failure. The converts seem few; the state's law is mostly unchanged. But when feminist legal scholarship is seen as part of the maintenance of a normative community, the bases for judgment are more complex. Feminist legal scholars have brought to light the narratives of the oppression of women, and by this work they have helped to maintain a community of women committed to the redemption of our world. They have also altered the dominant discourse about women in our culture and thus contributed to the surest source of meaningful law reform. In the face of a mostly unrepentant state, they have achieved much.

The Possibility of Redemption

Feminist legal scholarship is work of despair and redemption. The despair arises from several interrelated considerations. First, the reality of domination is personal and powerful to these scholars. Second, the roots of that domination could hardly run deeper. Faced with such a harsh specter, feminists would seem to have only a limited number of moves.

It may seem, as a practical matter, that they cannot make the move to insularity. They cannot pretend to retreat to a world apart from the oppression since for them no such world exists. As a practical matter, there is no place where the conditions of gender discrimination are wholly absent.[21] Thus, for feminist legal scholars, and for women generally, the obvious choices are to despair or to pursue a redemptive vision.

On the other hand, women do have moves that are insular in quality. While a retreat to a distinct place free of law's and man's oppression seems impractical, women can, and do, turn away from the state's law in various particular ways. Women's shelters for abused women and their children constitute communities of temporary and partial refuge from the violence of men, providing a security not given by the state's law and the police agents of the state. The turn to self-induced abortion, whether by the drug RU 486 or by "menstrual extraction," is another example of an insular move. As the constitutional protection for abortion erodes and the regulatory laws become ever more intrusive, the use of agents of self-induced abortion, and the advocacy and teaching of those methods, constitute a turning away from the law that seeks to restrict or deny abortions. Women say, in effect, "We need not change the state's law, we may simply render it irrelevant for us."

The state, of course, can be expected to counter any such move.

The state has resisted the importation of RU 486; and other means of self-induced abortion, if they become too visible and significant a response, will likely become the subject of coercive intervention. Feminists, as is true for the members of each normative community that stands in opposition to the state, will engage in a range of evolving responses to the state's ever-changing law.

Although there are many powerful examples of despair and redemption in feminist legal scholarship, I have chosen to return to the work of Susan Estrich. As discussed in Chapter 1, Estrich's article on rape begins with her own story. "Eleven years ago, a man held an ice pick to my throat and said: 'Push over, shut up, or I'll kill you.' I did what he said, but I couldn't stop crying. A hundred years later, I jumped out of my car as he drove away."[22] Her choice to begin this way is important. At the time of writing, she was a Harvard Law School professor, and the paper appeared in a prestigious journal of legal scholarship. In addition to telling of the racist and sexist assumptions of the police, Estrich wrote of the stigma that attaches to the victims of rape.

> At first, it is something you simply don't talk about. Then it occurs to you that people whose houses are broken into or who are mugged in Central Park talk about it all the time. Rape is a much more serious crime. If it isn't my fault, why am I supposed to be ashamed? If I shouldn't be ashamed, if it wasn't "personal," why look askance when I mention it?[23]

She acknowledges the significance of this stigma by choosing to begin her paper with a statement that she knows will startle the reader precisely because we do not expect her to so directly reveal her own experience of victimization.

From this beginning narrative, the balance of her work is freighted with its meaning, and Estrich intersperses stories of other rapes in her analysis of the law of rape. Estrich tells the story of *State vs. Alston*, a 1984 North Carolina case.[24] In *Alston* the woman had been living with her assailant but moved out because he had been physically abusive. Some time later, the man intercepted her at her school and grabbed her by the arm.

> At one point, the defendant told the victim he was going to "fix" her face; when told that their relationship was over, the defendant stated that he had a "right" to have sex with her again. The two went to the house of a friend. The defendant asked her if she was "ready," and the victim told him she did not want to have sexual relations. The defendant pulled her up from the chair, undressed her, pushed her legs apart, and penetrated her. She cried. [25]

The North Carolina Supreme Court reversed the defendant's conviction, concluding that even while viewing the evidence in the light most favorable to the prosecution there was insufficient evidence of "force," an element of the crime of rape. The grabbing of the woman's arm, the history of physical abuse, and the threat to "fix" her face were all irrelevant. Although such acts may have made her fearful, the court found them insufficient because, in the judge's sense of things, the force and threat were not directly applied to induce the act of intercourse. Estrich notes, "The undressing and the pushing of her legs apart . . . were not even mentioned as factors to be considered." [26]

The North Carolina Supreme Court applied the law of *Alston* in *State v. Lester*, a subsequent rape case in which the defendant was the father of the fifteen-year-old victim. [27] Estrich tells the story:

> Prior to the parents' divorce, the defendant frequently beat the children's mother in the [children's] presence. . . . He had a gun and on one occasion pointed it at his children. He engaged in sexual activity with all three of his daughters. . . . [The] mother found out and confronted the defendant. He swore never to touch [the daughter] again, and then threatened to kill both mother and daughter if they told anyone of his actions. On both of the occasions in question, the victim ini-

tially refused her father's demand to take her clothes off and "do it." In both cases, she complied when the demand was repeated and she sensed that her father was becoming angry. The court held that the defendant could be convicted of incest, but not of rape. [28]

The court somehow concluded that although there was evidence that the intercourse had been against the will of the daughter, there was insufficient evidence of forcible rape.

> In the instant case there is evidence that the acts of sexual intercourse between defendant and his fifteen-year-old daughter . . . were against her will. There is no evidence, however, that defendant used either actual or constructive force to accomplish the acts with which he is charged. As *Alston* makes clear, the victim's fear of defendant, however justified by his previous conduct, is insufficient to show that defendant *forcibly* raped his daughter. [29]

Estrich uses the stories of *Alston* and *Lester* in two ways. First, she points out that the cases can be criticized on doctrinal grounds.

> The courts' unwillingness to credit the victim's past experience of violence at the hands of the defendant stands in sharp contrast to the black letter law that a defendant's knowledge of his attacker's reputation for violence or ownership of a gun is relevant to the reasonableness of his use of deadly force in self-defense. [30]

The "element of force" in rape could be constructed to include the force that a man exerts when he demands sex in the face of verbal resistance, the implicit force that arises from a history of abuse, and the manifested force of shoving a woman's legs apart to penetrate her. Or, instead, the element of force can be interpreted, as by this court, to mean the direct application of actual physical force beyond the force of the intercourse itself, which was absent in these two cases.

If judges make assumptions about how difficult it is to determine the consensual quality of a woman's participation in intercourse, if they contrast the "de minimis" violation of penetration with the "real" violation of assault, it is easy for them to conclude that there was no *forcible* rape. If, on the other hand, a judge were to bring to the case a sympathetic reading of the stories told by Estrich, a very different sense of the element of force in rape law might emerge. This is the second thing Estrich does — she provides some new stories that may, or may not, become part of society's understanding of what rape means.

Estrich does one other, powerful thing in the recounting of the experiences of the women victims in *Alston* and *Lester* — she connects them with her own story.

> I am not at all sure how the judges who decided *Alston* would explain the victim's simultaneous refusal to consent and failure to resist. For myself, it is not at all difficult to understand that a woman who had been repeatedly beaten, who had been a passive victim of both violence and sex during the "consensual" relationship, who had sought to escape from the man, who is confronted and threatened by him, who summons the courage to tell him their relationship is over only to be answered by his assertion of a "right" to sex — a woman in such a position would not fight. She wouldn't fight; she might cry. Hers is the reaction of "sissies" in playground fights. Hers is the reaction of people who have already been beaten, or who never had the power to fight in the first instance. Hers is, from my reading, the most common reaction of women to rape. It certainly was mine.[31]

Despite the advent of rape shield laws that restrict the introduction of evidence of the victim's sexual history, the elimination of the spousal exemption in many states, and other apparent reforms, rape victims, especially those who are not "real" rape victims, are still essentially put on trial themselves.[32] Law reform falters because the legal elements of "consent" and "force," as conceived by police officers, prosecutors, judges, and juries, are freighted with the meanings of the dominant culture — the meanings of men's stories.

While rape shield laws may bar the introduction of testimony about the woman's sexual history for the blunt purpose of impugning her character, the legal issue of consent and the legal definition of requisite force allow certain assumptions to shape the outcome of these cases. The point is not that changes in the rules do not matter. Rape shield laws and the elimination of spousal exemption have made a difference. On the other hand, the adoption of so called "fresh complaint" rules that require a rape victim to report the crime within a specified time period have made another kind of difference. In any event, in Estrich's words, "the problem has never been the words of the statutes as much as the interpretation of them."[33] So long as the officers of the state are inclined to see a rape victim as a willing participant turned spiteful liar, or as a provocateur, or simply as a woman who carelessly put herself in harm's way, the meaning of rape law will be shaped by these stories.

Rape shield laws may keep out evidence of the victim's sexual history, but the relevance of that evidence has always come from a willingness to accept a portrayal of the woman as spiteful liar or provocateur. So long as these images have currency, we can expect to see their influence in the law. For example, the evidentiary focus will shift to the absence of physical evidence of violent assault, or to some other evidence that connects with these images. After all, the sexual history that is excluded by the rape shield law always drew its influence from the underlying idea of the woman as sexually compliant lover turned spiteful liar. So long as judges and jurors hold such ideas in their minds, they are likely to see corroboration in the testimony of the witnesses and in the demeanor of the victim. When William Kennedy Smith was tried for rape several years ago, his lawyers fought for the admissibility of the victim's bra as evidence, just as the prosecution fought to keep it out.[34] In theory, the intact bra was relevant to the issue of force; in reality, the delicate, "sexy" quality of the bra was what the defense wanted the jury to see and what the prosecution wanted to keep from the jury. What the lawyers on each side knew was that the jury would bring certain assumptions of their own to this piece of physical evidence.

Nonetheless, rape law changes. For example, the North Carolina Supreme Court changed the precepts of its rape law in a series of cases following *Alston* and *Lester*. In a 1987 case, *State v. Strickland*, the North Carolina Supreme Court, citing Estrich's article and noting her critical reading of the *Alston* case, cast doubt on the reach of the *Alston* rule.[35] Subsequent decisions by the court severely limit the precedential value of *Alston*. It now appears that in North Carolina a well-grounded fear of the defendant may satisfy the "force element" unless a prior history of sexual relations exists.

In another rape case, *State v. Etheridge*, decided one month after *Strickland*, the court reconsidered *Lester*.[36] In *Etheridge* the defendant was convicted of raping his twelve-year-old daughter and thirteen-year-old son. The defendant relied on the "general fear" rule of *Alston*, as extended to the alleged rape of a minor in the *Lester* case, arguing that his children's fear of him was not enough to satisfy the "force element." The court expressly overruled *Lester*, noting that "sexual activity between a parent and minor child is not comparable to sexual activity between two adults with a history of consensual intercourse." The court again cited Estrich's work.

The North Carolina Supreme Court's reconsideration of its rape jurisprudence reveals both the power and the limits of work like Estrich's. *Lester* is overruled; the "general fear" rule is unavailable in North Carolina if one rapes a child. The court strictly limits the precedential import of *Alston*. Still, the North Carolina Supreme Court is unwilling simply to kill off *Alston* by expressly overruling it. The court also continues to attach great significance to a prior history of sexual relations and remains unwilling to see the unwanted physical penetration of a woman as a sufficient act of force. The court remains committed to the idea that if a man and a woman have previously engaged in consensual sex, that man may pull off her clothes, push her legs apart, and penetrate her body while the woman explicitly says no, and still not have committed rape because the "element of force" is absent. Some things changed in North Carolina rape law — apparently due in part to the influence of Estrich's work — yet much remains the same.

Vinson, Rabidue, and Sexual Harassment

Susan Estrich has taught us some similar lessons about the law of sexual harassment in the workplace. Through the decisions of the courts and the policies of the Equal Employment Opportunity Commission (EEOC), a federal cause of action under the federal statute called Title VII for workplace sexual harassment has emerged.[37] The U.S. Supreme Court acknowledged the existence of the cause of action in 1986 in *Meritor Savings Bank v. Vinson*.[38] In the *Vinson* case the Court recognized both the "quid pro quo" cause of action in which sex is demanded as a condition of the job, as well as the "hostile environment" cause of action in which the woman can show the existence of a hostile working environment arising from verbal or physical conduct of a sexual nature.

Estrich's article "Sex at Work" shows how the apparent victory in the *Vinson* case is not likely to provide women with meaningful remedies for a sexually hostile working environment.[39] The essential problem with the hostile environment cause of action arises from the Court's creation of the element of "unwelcomeness."[40] Although consent by the woman is not an issue in the hostile environment cause of action, she must show that the advances at issue were unwelcome. This element shifts the focus to the behavior of the woman, with courts allowing the defendant employer to introduce evidence about her "sexually provocative speech or dress." Thus a woman who wears tight clothing and uses sexually explicit words supposedly "welcomes" a working environment in which male employees proposition her, call her demeaning names, and put photos of nude women on the walls. By the manipulation of this element, lawyers can transform a claim brought by a woman against her employer into a trial of the woman's virtue and an inquiry into whether she "asked for" the sexual comments and contact that the men imposed on her in the workplace.

In the *Vinson* case, the woman employee, a bank teller, was subjected to repeated sexual advances from her supervisor. Estrich described the environment in the following terms:

> At first, she refused, but, afraid of losing her job, she eventually agreed. Over the next three years, Taylor repeatedly demanded sexual relations with Vinson. She testified that she had intercourse with him forty or fifty times. He fondled her in front of other employees, followed her into the women's rest room, exposed himself to her, and forcibly raped her on several occasions.[41]

The unwelcomeness element invites the judge and jury to wonder whether Mechelle Vinson "welcomed" this treatment by her supervisor. And in figuring this out, the judge and jury, with the defense lawyer's encouragement, may consider whether Ms. Vinson wore tight sweaters or short skirts. This is the federal law of sexual harassment in action.

The unwelcomeness element in sexual harassment law draws its coherence from certain stories about women — stories of women with a repressed desire for dirty talk, or simple stories about the office "slut." It is also a piece of substantive law that stands as an invitation for judges and juries to import their versions of these stories into the litigation brought by a woman employee who has experienced some version of Vinson's nightmare.

Estrich shows how the definition of a hostile environment can reflect this process. She tells the facts of *Rabidue v. Osceola Refining Co.*,[42] a 1986 federal appellate court decision:

According to the dissenting judge, pictures of nude and scantily clad women abounded, including one, which hung on a wall for eight years, of a woman with a golf ball on her breasts and a man with his golf club, standing over her and yelling "fore." The language was equally offensive: One co-worker, never disciplined despite repeated complaints, routinely referred to women as "whores," "cunts," and "pussy." But the Sixth Circuit found all this de minimis.[43]

A majority of a federal court appeals panel accepted the trial court's judgment that these acts were "de minimis." These judges necessarily brought to bear a set of narratives about women and the workplace not shared by the objecting women employees.

Similarly, Estrich shows how the quid pro quo cause of action provides little real hope for the woman employee. The typical "quid pro quo" plaintiff has been fired, because she alleges, she refused to have sex with a male supervisor. She must prove that the supervisor demanded sex and that he fired her for her refusal. These elements seem obvious and not problematic. Estrich demonstrates, however, the ways in which these formal elements, as actually applied, hinder women seeking relief for sexual harassment.

Male supervisors typically do not send memos expressing their sexual demands, thus proving the demand itself is often difficult. Even when the quid pro quo advance by the man is proven, the employer typically asserts apparently legitimate reasons for the woman's dismissal: her work was deficient, she was habitually tardy, she had difficulty working with others, and so on. The subjective quality of employee evaluation permits a range of reasons to be offered, none of which can easily be disproven.

Neither the unwelcomeness element in the hostile environment cause of action nor the basic elements of the quid pro quo case are facially unreasonable legal principles. They allow, however, the importation of all kinds of stories told about women at work. So long as stories about women secretly enjoying "erotic" posters and "rough" sex have currency in our culture, the laws of rape and sexual harassment, as applied, will provide only limited shelter for women.

Susan Estrich and other feminist legal scholars have shown us the deep-rooted source of our gender discrimination problem and the severe limitations of law reform. There is without doubt a despairing quality to the work. On the other hand, by telling new stories, hers and those of other women, Estrich is using her power as a writer to make new law. Each reader hears her stories. Even as she recounts the explanation for the limits of law reform, she is engaged in discourse that would yield a truly changed law of rape. She cannot make any reader adopt her stories as their own, but to the extent that any reader does so, the law's meaning — the combination of rules and narratives — is changed.

Similarly, Estrich's work on sexual harassment is both despairing and redemptive. She shows how the ostensible victory of the *Vinson* case is hollow, yet her stories of sex at work can affect the meaning of the unwelcomeness element in the law. Imagine two judges, one of whom embraces some version of the assumption that women secretly enjoy dirty talk, and the other embracing Estrich's narratives as accurate depictions of the experience of women. Although both judges will accept the abstract legal principle that a legally actionable hostile environment must be unwelcome, each is likely to attach different meanings to the concept of unwelcomeness.

The doctrinal dirty work of "force" in rape and "unwelcomeness" in sexual harassment has always been a product of the discourse and narratives that surround these words. After all, the absence of force is a coherent defense to a charge of rape, and a hostile environment sensibly does not arise when a woman welcomes the behavior that creates the environment. The error is in the legal meaning that emerges from stories about women and sex.

Reform of the formal precepts of law, on the other hand, is not pointless. First, women do benefit from the application of the new precepts. Rape shield laws spare victims at least some of the pain and humiliation that was routine under the old laws. Repeal of the spousal exception allows women at least the possibility of charging a husband with rape. Women experiencing sexual harassment at work can employ Title VII. Moreover, the very existence of sexual harassment causes of action provides incentives for employers to pay some attention to workplace conditions in a way not demanded by the old precepts. These gains, however, can be easily overstated, as the work of scholars such as Estrich suggests.

Most importantly, the process of law reform can also help women by generating different cultural narratives about women and their lives. The process of reforming rape law generated important new stories about the abuse that rape victims have suffered within the legal system. These stories were not widely known before the advent of rape shield laws.

To the extent law reform brings forth new narratives that are assimilated by those who administer the law, women's lives under law will change. To the extent reform only changes the formal rules, leaving in place the old stories about women, women's lives under law will look more like the old reality and less like the new vision.

Feminist legal scholars have told us stories of despair as a means of working towards our redemption. In judging their work, Robert Cover's appraisal of the nineteenth-century abolitionist movement seems apt:

> While their movement lasted, the radical constitutionalists contributed to an immense growth in law. They worked out a constitutional attack on slavery from the general structure of the Constitution; they evolved a literalist attack from the language of the due process clause and from the jury and grand jury provisions of the fifth and sixth amendments; they studied interpretive methodologies and self-consciously employed the one most favorable to their ends; they devel-

oped arguments for extending the range of constitutional sources to include at least the Declaration of Independence. Their pamphlets, arguments, columns, and books constitute an important part of the legal literature on slavery, which, I believe, would substantially eclipse contemporaneous writings in, say, American tort law. . . . In the workings of a committed community with common symbols and discourse, common narratives and interpretation, the law undeniably grew.[44]

Feminist legal scholars have also contributed to an immense growth in law. They have enriched legal thought with innovative arguments and methodologies, they have produced a body of literature that would eclipse the legal literature in most doctrinal areas, and they have contributed to real change in the law. Their narratives have entered the realm of discourse beyond their own community and will have an unknowable but potentially powerful influence.

Roe, Planned Parenthood, and Abortion

Law is meaning executed through commitment. Interpretation without a willingness to act on that interpretation may be the derivation of meaning but it is not *legal* meaning. No law can exist without commitment.

The centrality of commitment in the construction of the law that affects women's lives is well revealed in the wrenching issue of abortion.[45] The feminist normative community shares the central precept of a woman's right to choose what happens to her body and thus the right to choose to end an unwanted pregnancy. The narratives of the community are about impregnation by coerced intercourse, whether by rape or by overbearing husbands; about hideous experiences of self-induced abortion or abortion by back room "butchers"; and about the context of gender oppression within which pregnancy and abortion arise.[46] The members of the feminist nomos bring their commitment to the meaning that arises from their precepts and narratives.

[127]

Yet those who seek to blockade the abortion clinics are also creating and advancing law. They share as their central precept the principle that any fetus is an innocent life that should not be taken by abortion. Their stories are often "told" pictorially. The use of pictures of aborted fetuses, or even the fetuses themselves, has been a persistent part of the discourse of the "pro-life" community. [47] The pictures reveal the resemblance between the fetus and the newborn infant, thus suggesting that abortion is analogous to infanticide. These activists also tell stories about the "happy" alternative of adoption. [48] And they act on their law; they back their interpretation with their commitment, and sometimes with their violence.

While these opposed normative communities show their commitment by their sometimes violent clashes at the barricades surrounding the abortion clinics, the Supreme Court shows only a shallow and divided commitment to its constitutional law of abortion. [49] Beginning with *Roe v. Wade*, the seminal 1973 decision, and continuing in the post-*Roe* abortion cases, the Court has demonstrated its inability to set forth a strong, coherent, and shared vision of law. [50] Justice Blackmun's opinion in *Roe* created legal meaning by using the Constitution to circumscribe the state's power to prohibit abortion. Yet the Court adopted neither community's competing vision of law. By circumscribing the state's power to prohibit abortion, the Court showed that it did not embrace the "pro-life" community's vision of law. On the other hand, the Court limited state power according to the trimesters of pregnancy, granting to the state the power to take the decision away from the woman at some temporal marking point before birth. In this sense, the feminist vision of law is likewise not fully accepted.

Many criticize the *Roe* opinion and its progeny as poorly constructed, incoherent or contradictory. In fact, the Court's decisions in abortion cases reflect a set of justices who either seek a compromise solution that grants the woman some limited autonomy or would turn loose state power to regulate, or even flatly forbid, abortions. Neither approach represents a strong, coherent vision of law.

The Court's 1992 abortion decision in *Planned Parenthood v. Casey* is a stunning example of the weak and mixed sense of constitutional law that the Court has embraced.[51] Justice O'Connor, writing the plurality opinion, initially expresses her fealty to *Roe*: "After considering the fundamental constitutional questions resolved by *Roe*, principles of institutional integrity, and the rule of stare decisis, we are led to conclude this: the essential holding of *Roe v. Wade* should be retained and once again reaffirmed."[52] Thereafter, she goes on to discard virtually all of the constitutional meaning that was created in *Roe*. The strict scrutiny standard is replaced by an "undue burden" standard that sanctions substantial and intrusive regulation that is explicitly intended to dissuade, discourage, and make more difficult a woman's choice to have an abortion. O'Connor dismisses the trimester structure because it gets in the way of her choice to extend the state's regulatory power all the way back to the moment of conception. And in the process she upholds virtually all of the Pennsylvania abortion law, a law that was simply and clearly inconsistent with the principles of *Roe*.

After *Planned Parenthood*, there is little commitment on the part of the Court that might restrict the deployment of state power against the choice of women to have abortions. On the other hand, no member of the Court seems willing to create constitutional law that would "protect innocent life." It is no wonder that both of the competing normative communities are angry and deeply critical of the Court's decisions.

Commitment is always the central part of law. In the abortion context, where the state's commitment is weak and confused, the significance of the commitment within the competing normative communities is increased. They each must turn to the political battleground of the state legislatures, where their success will turn on not just the number of voters each group commands but also on the intensity and depth of commitment of their members.

In the abortion context, the commitment of those who hold a particular vision of law is also especially important because the weakness of the Court's commitment creates a kind of vacuum within which each competing nomos has a special opportunity to see their vision realized. When the state has a strong commitment and stands ready to exercise its imperfect monopoly on violence to impose its law, the commitment of opposed normative communities is expressed through resistance, civil disobedience, or denunciation. The state's opposition typically overshadows the community's vision of law as a loud noise overshadows a quiet sound. But in the abortion context, the Court's weak commitment means that there is no overshadowing effect. The competing normative communities each advance their vision of law and seek the realization of their law as the state's law. The noises they make are the only ones to be heard.

As the "pro-life" community and the "pro-choice" community advance their competing visions of law — one a vision of the protection of innocent life, the other a vision of women's autonomy — they participate in a special moment in our history. The law of abortion for the twenty-first century may be a patchwork quilt of differing state laws or the result of a national consensus imposed by federal law, or something else. But whatever form it takes, that law will be a product of the commitment of the competing normative communities.

An Unruly Moment

So long as we see feminist scholarship as advocacy, we can easily accommodate it, whether we stand as sympathizers or critics. As critics we can dismiss the work because of its unconventional methods or judge it to be a weak rhetorical effort because of its limited influence on law and its apparent failure to convert its critics. As sympathizers, we can express our support and suppose that we have done all that we can sensibly do.

Yet the moment we see feminist scholarship and its law through the ideas of precept, narrative, and commitment, everything changes. We see that this body of scholarship is part of the maintenance of a community of committed individuals who share basic precepts and the narratives that supply legal meaning. This work does not take the form of the rhetoric of the state's apologists precisely because feminist scholarship is part of an altogether different activity. Most importantly, the use of stories is not a rhetorical gambit, it is the essential teaching of the shared narratives of the normative community. Precisely because the state's narratives, or those of opposed normative communities, are out there in the discourse of society, the feminist must keep telling and retelling her stories in order to maintain the community and to work toward redemption.

Thus feminist scholarship cannot be judged simply by its influence. It stands as part of a nomic enterprise. As with normative communities that have preceded it, the judgment of history will be more complex. Whatever that judgment, feminist legal scholarship will stand as a remarkable body of teachings, a rich set of stories, and an imaginative reconstitution of law.

All of which brings us to the essential point. The choice for us is much harder than we would like to imagine, especially for those who would cast themselves as being in solidarity with a feminist agenda. The struggle that is currently being played out at the abortion clinic barricades and before the Supreme Court — and in the courtrooms, bedrooms, and workplaces of this country — is no mere matter of words. In this struggle there is no sensible position of solidarity from the outside, as an observer, anymore than there is a sensible position of solidarity for any bystander to a violent struggle. Because this is a struggle by a nomos facing at once the violence of the state's law and the commitment of opposing normative communities, solidarity does not come so cheap.

The unavoidable choice for us is the one that every normative community poses for anyone who would claim its law as their law. Each person must take sides, or stake out his or her own normative vision. If one wishes to take the side of the feminist nomos, one must enter it to the degree that one can. Hearing the stories is a beginning. Accepting those stories as real and important is an essential part of the process.

Each of us must determine the degree and nature of our commitment to the vision of law that emerges from the precepts and narratives of our own normative universe. Even when that commitment simply takes the form of verbal opposition to other, competing visions of law, we need to see it as a matter of commitment. In choosing the degree of our commitment we must discern the commitment of the state. Not everyone is prepared to be a martyr to his vision of law. Yet each one of us must understand that some version of the martyr's commitment is always demanded of anyone who seeks to live a life of reflection and integrity. If we understand feminist scholarship and its law in these terms, we see that the price of true solidarity with the feminist nomos is high indeed. While our individual commitment may not be written in blood, we cannot pretend that this is a bloodless matter.

As we approach the new millennium, we see a political and social landscape that is radically unstable. The formal legal institutions are busy making new law, including the much-heralded "welfare reform" that is explicitly and punitively directed at women. It is truly an unruly moment in history, and for women — especially for those in poverty and for black women — a disturbing time. At every moment, but especially at such an unruly moment, the questions for all of us are simply put. To what normative vision of law are we committed, and what is the depth of our commitment?

5

Despair and Redemption

Throughout this book I have used the term "narrative" to describe some of the basic building blocks of the state's law: narratives of women as secretly desiring dirty talk on the job, narratives of blacks as seeking special unearned advantages, narratives of poor people as shirking work. I have argued that these narratives are inapt. Most women really mean no when they say it. Most blacks seek the sense of independence and self-esteem that comes from doing useful work. And poor people are not inherently prone to theft, at least not to any degree greater than stockbrokers, doctors, bankers, or lawyers. Thus it might seem that the basic problem identified in this book is one of a collective mistake — we have somehow embraced a mistaken set of narratives and thereby constructed some bad law. This, however, misstates the problem.

The justices of the Supreme Court in the late nineteenth century sanctioned apartheid. This law was in part a product of the narratives they possessed of blacks as inherently different and less worthy, that is, the stories of racism. These were dominant narratives in the society out of which these justices came. Their culture taught and otherwise reinforced these stories.

By embracing the narratives of racism, nineteenth-century

Americans gave coherence to law that avoided the risk and change that would come with a breakdown of the formal separation of the races. They preserved for themselves the security of their familiar world. They kept this for themselves by the subjugation of innocent people. The basic tool for subjugation was law and the law's necessary coherence came from narratives and assumptions that were in an inescapable sense chosen and not merely received. They were chosen because they worked for the dominant race, even though they propped up a social structure that humiliated and subjugated innocent human beings. Thus, these narratives, like the law they built, were a reflection of the dominant moral values of nineteenth-century America.

Our time and our narratives exhibit a similar quality. When, for example, we compose the law of sexual harassment out of stories of women as secretly welcoming certain behaviors, whatever their stated preferences, we are not merely failing to apprehend reality. Nor do we merely find ourselves in possession of a set of stories that we passively received. We are exhibiting our choice not to accord to women the same measure of respect and the same assumption of autonomy as we give to men. We are showing that we see women as different from men and less worthy. And we choose one set of narratives over another because they work for the politically, economically, and socially dominant gender. They help us — men in particular — hold on to a familiar and comfortable world in much the same way that the nineteenth-century narratives helped whites hold on to their familiar and comfortable world of racial apartheid.

While "narrative" may be an apt term for the assumptions and imaginings out of which legal meaning is derived, the term also refers to the moral values of a given society. When we build the law out of such narratives as those described above, we are not merely mistaken in our apprehension, we are maintaining or constructing a world through the power of the state's law. We embrace our narratives in part because we were taught them by our culture. But we hold on to them in part because they give coherence to a world that we desperately want to preserve.

In the struggle for the content of the state's law that will govern the lives of blacks, women, and the poor, the possibility that a real hearing of their experiences will bring about a shift in narratives and corresponding shift in law is a recurring hope. In every time, the cause of the outsider has triggered eloquence.

Still, the state's law has remained largely unaffected by the "counter-narratives" that swirl around it. The 1896 Supreme Court case *Plessy v. Ferguson*, which we have discussed in depth, provides a powerful example. The briefs filed by the lawyers challenging the Louisiana law vividly depicted the racism that was the motive for, and the message of, the law. For example, the brief of S. F. Phillips and F. D. McKenney reads in part, "[The Louisiana law] amounts to a *taunt by law* of that previous condition of [slavery] — a taunt by the State, to be administered with perpetually repeated like taunts *in word* by railroad employees [emphasis in the original]."[1]

The brief of James C. Walker and Albion W. Tourgee provided the most evocative of the outsider narratives. The lawyers concluded their brief with this remarkable imagining:

> Suppose a member of this court, nay, suppose every member of it, by some mysterious dispensation of providence should wake tomorrow with a black skin and curly hair — the two obvious and controlling indications of race — and in traveling through that portion of the country where the "Jim Crow Car" abounds, should be ordered into it by the conductor. . . . What humiliation; what rage would then fill the judicial mind! How would the resources of language not be taxed in objurgation! Why would this sentiment prevail in your minds? Simply because you would then feel and know that such assortment of the citi-

zens on the line of race was a discrimination intended to humiliate and degrade the former subject and dependent class — an attempt to perpetuate the caste distinctions on which slavery rested — a statute in the words of the Court "tending to reduce the colored people of the country to the condition of a subject race." . . . Because it does this, the statute is a violation of . . . the Fourteenth Amendment.[2]

The lawyers thereby invited the justices to fill their imagination with a story that would reveal the undeniable purpose and effect of the law and thus the constitutional violation it embodied.

Nonetheless, the *Plessy* Court constitutionally validated the law, advancing the outrageous "self-imposed stigma" doctrine:

> We consider the underlying fallacy of plaintiff's argument to consist in the assumption that the enforced separation of the two races stamps the colored race with a badge of inferiority. If this be so, it is not by reason of anything found in the act, but solely because the colored race chooses to put that construction upon it.[3]

The sad truth is that the telling of counter-narratives is likely to have little impact on the state's law. Part of the reason for this pessimistic view flows from the fact that in one way or another, judges, legislators, and other lawmakers are tied to the interests of the dominant class. The notable exceptions, crusading judges and maverick legislators, prove the general rule.

This linkage is a product of corrupting relationships like campaign financing. But, more importantly, the linkage is a matter of natural affiliation. Lawmakers, whether judges or legislators, come mostly from the ranks of the dominant class — white, male, higher socioeconomic strata. To expect them to set aside the narratives and corresponding values of their own class is asking a lot. (This is the basic logic both of the liberals' efforts to diversify the federal judiciary and draw legislative districts so as to enhance the probability of minority representation, and of the conservatives' resistance to just such diversification.)

Focusing on judges, another reason for pessimism about change through counter-narratives arises. Judges, by culturally ascribed role, are priests not prophets; their job is to serve and maintain the state's law and not to "make law." On the one hand, they exercise judgment and make choices; on the other hand, judges understand that their role is formally subservient to the law. For example, judges often exercise choice in their interpretation of a statute, yet a judge's role precludes explicit disavowal of an applicable and concededly constitutional statute. In *Justice Accused*, Robert Cover described the nature of judicial self-abnegation:

> The inclination to conceive of the judicial role as one of will-less, self-abnegating application of law . . . was the result neither of a failure to appreciate the creative input of the judiciary, nor of a failure to understand the limitless bounds of discretion and of its exercise. Rather, the self-abnegation was the very product of the realization that judicial input was inevitable, substantial, and controversial. . . . The judge knew he made law. . . . Yet he felt, and rightly so, that he was more constrained than free; that he made law differently than did legislators, and that the difference was a qualitative one.[4]

Although Cover was describing a set of judges of the last century, the idea applies with as much force to the self-conception of contemporary judges.

Judges are surely not legal automatons. Thoughtful judges have always understood the inescapable element of choice that defines their work. Yet to suppose that law is politics and that judges are simply free actors who profess to a wholly false sense of constraint in order to mask their power misses the mark as well. Judges take seriously their responsibility and demonstrate this by their tendency to self-abnegation. Judges are both free and constrained at once.

When, for example, the justices in the poverty cases we have discussed uttered the litany of helplessness and argued that the legal issue resided beyond the boundaries of their jurisdiction, they were tapping into the theme of judicial self-abnegation. Those who seek to redeem the law of poverty by the telling of counter-narratives face two problems when their stories are directed to judges. First, they face the problem common to all lawmakers, the ingrained resistance to narratives that would shatter the familiar world of the law. Second, these storytellers face the special problem of countering the tendency of judges to self-abnegation.

When Thurgood Marshall argued before the Court in *Brown v. Board of Education*, he faced two barriers. First, he had to help the justices imagine the world of apartheid from the vantage point of black children and families. His task and his methods mirrored those of Albion Tourgee, the *Plessy* lawyer. Unlike Tourgee, Marshall apparently succeeded. But Marshall also had to persuade the justices to overrule *Plessy*.

Legal scholars know that courts engage in extraordinary intellectual legerdemain to avoid overruling a prior case, a precedent. This phenomenon has led many to the conclusion that judges are essentially political actors pretending to a false sense of constraint — that they first choose to kill off the old law and thereafter conjure the appearance of survival, as a murderer might prop up a victim's body in a chair and stick a newspaper in its hands. (The least examination, in either case, would reveal the true act of extinction.) In reality, judges typically have coherent explanations for why the law they create today is consistent with the old law. And judges often bow to the old law even when they would wish to choose otherwise.

The fact that judges always exercise judgment and choice and sometimes reject the received precedents does not mean that the notion of *stare decisis* — to stand by decided matters — is not a real and powerful idea. Judges seek a foundation for choice apart from their personal will. This foundation is to be found in what is already there and in what has been. They look backward, seeking the foundation. When they look backward, they see old law, old narratives.

To ask a judge to hear and embrace new narratives is to ask him or her to act on personal will and set aside the ascribed role of self-abnegation. The agent of law's redemption thus has good reason to doubt the power of counter-narratives.

This book focuses on the ways in which the state's law draws its coherence from dominant cultural narratives about blacks, women, and poor people as different and less worthy. We have focused on the interpretive side of law, and the basic raw material of this book has been judicial opinions.

A judicial opinion is an odd text. Different legal cultures demand different kinds of textual artifacts from their judges, or no text at all. Within our legal culture, we expect judges, except those at the lower level trial courts, to produce opinions. These opinions typically do several things. First, they announce the exercise of power, declaring who wins what. But if this were all they had to do, these texts would be much shorter than they typically are.

The bulk of the text of a typical judicial opinion appears to be devoted to the function of persuasion. Judges seek to persuade the reader of the correctness of their choices, although they understand that such persuasion is often elusive or unnecessary. It is elusive because any particular reader may be unmoved; no judicial opinion, even one authored by the most eloquent of his colleagues, could have persuaded Justice Marshall that the death penalty was constitutional. And, in a way, persuasion is not necessary because no one gets to vote on whether to accept the judge's choice or not; even judges who are popularly elected, and thus subject to popular approval of their performance, must know that virtually no one reads their opinions, apart from a relatively minuscule segment of their constituency. Undoubtedly, judges would like to imagine that their readers are persuaded. But self-aware judges know that this is often not the case.

Judicial opinions are also devoted to a related but somewhat less

ambitious sort of persuasion. Judges hope that even those who disagree will see that a given choice is a coherent exercise of judicial
power that falls within the boundaries of the judicial role. Thus
judges typically use the syllogistic, abstract analysis that is expected of them. They take great pains to construct an intellectual
foundation for the choice made. Some opinions are elegant intellectual structures, others are simply incoherent. Yet virtually every judicial opinion aspires to persuade the reader that the interpretive
activity is a reasonable, if not correct, exercise of intellect.

All of this describes the overriding quality of judicial opinions — their cold, abstract, and relentlessly logical tone. Exceptions of course exist, most commonly in dissenting opinions; the
reader, every once in a great while, will find passion, anger, and the
vivid depiction of the case's story.

However, the abstract tone of virtually all judicial opinions and
the intellectual energy devoted to the construction and the de-
construction of those opinions — including the work done in this
book — can be misleading. To the observer, debates among judges
via their opinions and debates among scholars through their scholarly writings resemble other intellectual battles. Argument about
the meaning of the Constitution's equal protection clause resembles
argument about the meaning of a poem by T. S. Eliot in that each
is an intellectual exercise in interpretation. But the student of law
who even roughly equates the two activities makes a grave error.

First, as most people understand, the consequences of the two
debates are radically different. Getting others to accept your interpretation of a poem may bring you prestige within a narrow circle.
Saying what shall be the meaning of the Constitution's equal protection clause in any particular case has a dramatic impact on the
lives and circumstances of human beings. The mother receiving
AFDC payments may be obliged to suffer the unannounced intrusion of government agents into her home because the state chooses

to so intrude and the judge says that nothing in the Constitution forbids such an exercise of the state's power.

Beyond this obvious difference in consequences is the inescapable connection between the interpretive activity in law and the activity of its enforcement. Hardly ever does a judicial opinion speak of its connection with violence. Analysts of judicial opinions also skate over this aspect of law. But every act of lawmaking — whether it is the interpretive activity of the judge or the precept-creating activity of the legislator, or the discretionary judgment of the welfare bureaucrat, or the on-the-street action of the police officer — is an action that summons the state to bring its violence to bear. Every such action is potentially written in blood. Most often, the individual acquiesces to the state without the actual deployment of violence. This acquiescence, however, is almost never a matter of intellectual persuasion. Very few losing litigants embrace the wisdom of the case's outcome. They go along because defiance is dangerous and generally futile.

As we read the intellectual artifacts of the law — opinions, legislative history, law journal articles — we can easily forget the violence that is the foundation of the state's law. An interpretation earns the name "state's law" precisely when the state signals its willingness to bring its violence to bear. This is not a bad thing; it is an inescapable thing. The state must act coercively. But we ought not to pretend that, for example, the black residents of Memphis, Tennessee, acquiesced in the state's construction of the wall insulating the all-white neighborhood from its unwanted black neighbors because they became persuaded of the correctness of the state's action and the Court's own acquiescence. Those black residents were presumably angry and unsatisfied. They chose not to tear down the wall because they imagined how the state would respond.

Whenever we debate and explore legal interpretation, we must know the essential nature of our inquiry. It is not merely a game of wits or just another intellectual exercise. We are debating the proper content of the state's law. And the state's law is a set of choices that we impose on others through violence.

Despair about the law is in part a product of one's expectations. I have taught many students over the past fifteen years. "The law" is almost always something different from what they expected. The most common myth they bring to their study is the idea of law as somehow just there, a given. They see their task as they probably saw much of their prior formal education, as the assimilation of data. Ideally, they will learn that law is humanly constructed and not given, that it is ceaselessly evolving and not fixed, and that thus their study of law must sensibly be about something other than the assimilation of the rules.

Some students experience another sort of change. They come to law school with the idea that law is inherently a set of wise and virtuous principles and that injustice is an aberrational and extra-legal phenomenon. Such students are appalled to discover that the law itself typically reflects the interests of the already powerful and that the law often has been, and still is, an instrument of subjugation and injustice. This discovery can lead to cynicism and despair.

Former students of Robert Cover tell me that he would tell them that "the railroad always wins." He meant that the law always reinforces and reflects the interests of the powerful and privileged. But, Cover taught, it was interesting and important to look for the explanations offered by the courts as to *why* the railroad was to win. In these explanations resided the hesitations, counter-values, and ideas that might form a small wedge in the state's law, a wedge that could be used to bring about a discrete and modest piece of justice on behalf of the less powerful members of our society. After all, the railroad does not always, *always* win.

If you approach the law supposing that it will protect the interests of the weak and the disenfranchised, and that it will blunt the power of the dominant interests, you will be a disappointed, even despairing, student of law. The brutal truth is that the law will in its general composition reflect the stories of the dominant class and their interests. And when those stories depict other people as different and less worthy, the law will embody such stereotypes.

I walk a fine line between hopeful cynicism and despair. I stay on the cynical but hopeful side of the line by recalling the work of those lawyers who fought, and fight, without self-delusion for law's reform. Thurgood Marshall, as lawyer and justice, never ceased his struggle, even though he had the clearest possible vision of law and of the world in which he lived. He was always attentive to the possibilities of driving a wedge through the state's law, creating a measure of justice and empathy. He was an irrepressible storyteller. And he was a man who did much good.

I do not know what lies ahead. My parents grew up in a time of racial apartheid. I grew up in a transitional period — the last years of formal apartheid merging into the era of civil rights, the War on Poverty, the feminist renewal. My children are growing up in a hard-to-define time. No separate water fountains, no "Help Wanted — Male" ads. Yet a time of "welfare reform" that envisions the starvation of others for no reason except that we have run out of patience and have decided that they are morally unworthy of our help. It is, perhaps happily, an unknowable future.

Notes

Chapter One

1. 18 Pa. Cons. Stat. Ann. §§ 3121 (1995).

2. By 1989, seventeen states had abrogated the spousal exemption by statute, and five by judicial opinion; however, five states had broadened their spousal exemptions to include nonmarried, cohabiting couples or mere social acquaintances. Anne L. Buckborough, comment entitled "Family Law: Recent Developments in the Law of Marital Rape," *1989 Annual Survey of American Law* 343 n. 4, 344 n. 5.

3. By 1989, forty-eight states, the military, and the federal government had enacted legislation restricting the admissibility of a victim's prior sexual history in rape proceedings. In the remaining states, Arizona and Utah, admissibility of prior sexual history was restricted by case law precedent. Kim Steinmetz, note on State v. Oliver entitled "Children With a Past: The Admissibility of the Victim's Prior Sexual Experience in Child Molestation Cases," *Arizona Law Review* 31 (1989): 680 nn. 18–19.

4. For an especially thoughtful exploration of this point, see Susan Estrich, *Real Rape* (Cambridge, Mass.: Harvard University Press, 1987).

5. Ibid., 1–2.

6. The legal academy has understood this at least since the rise of the "American legal realists" in the 1920s and 1930s. See Laura Kalman, *Legal Realism at Yale, 1927–1960* (Chapel Hill, N.C.: University of North Carolina Press, 1986). The contemporary "critical legal studies" movement in legal academics has taken this theme and given it a leftist political spin. See "A Bibliography of Critical Legal Studies," Duncan Kennedy and Karl E. Klare, eds., *Yale Law Journal* 94 (1984): 461.

7. As this book will demonstrate, the idea that judges can somehow simply apply some externally given set of rules called law and avoid the exercise of choice grounded in values is lunatic; the real agenda in the fight over the composition of the federal judiciary has been about ideology, and this has been true for both Republican and Democratic nominees.

8. See "Nobill in Rape Case Prompts Outrage: Suspect Wore a Condom at Woman's Request," *Houston Chronicle*, 10 October 1992, A-30; and Judy Mann, "Beyond the Risk of Rape," *Washington Post*, 16 October 1992, E-3.

9. See Christy Hoppe, "Rapist Gets 40 Years: Consent Defense in Condom Case Unsuccessful," *Dallas Morning News*, 15 May 1993, A-33; and "40-year Sentence for Defendant in 'Condom Rape' Conviction," *Los Angeles Times*, 15 May 1993, A-2.

10. Robert Cover, "The Supreme Court, 1982 Term — Foreword: Nomos and Narrative," *Harvard Law Review* 97 (1983): 4.

11. Increasingly, legal scholars have demonstrated their understanding of the essential connections between narrative and the law. Not surprisingly, most of these scholars are themselves women and members of racial minorities. In particular, I have benefited from reading the extraordinary work of Derrick Bell, Richard Delgado, and Patricia Williams.

12. Cover, "Nomos and Narrative," 4.

13. Plessy v. Ferguson, 163 U.S. 537 (1896). See Charles A. Lofgren, *The Plessy Case: A Legal-Historical Interpretation* (New York: Oxford University Press, 1987).

14. Grant Gilmore, *The Ages of American Law* (New Haven: Yale University Press, 1977), 110–11.

Chapter Two

1. See Robert Ferguson, "Holmes and the Judicial Figure," *University of Chicago Law Review* 55 (1988): 517.

2. Dred Scott v. Sandford, 60 U.S. 393 (1856).

3. The work of Professor George M. Fredrickson on the history and nature of racism is especially illuminating; see his books *The Black Image in the White Mind* (New York: Harper and Row, 1971) and *The Arrogance of Race* (Middletown, Conn.: Wesleyan University Press, 1988). His essay "Masters and Mudsills: The Role of Race in the Planter Ideology of South Carolina," to be found in the latter work, powerfully describes a particular metaphorical version of racism.

4. Hammond quoted in Fredrickson, *The Arrogance of Race*, 23.

5. *The Pro-Slavery Argument as Maintained by the Most Distinguished Writers of the Southern States, Containing the Several Essays on the Subject of Chancellor Harper, Governor Hammond, Dr. Simms, and Professor Dew* (New York: Negro Universities Press, 1968), 354.

6. See Fredrickson, *The Arrogance of Race*, 15–27.

7. Plessy v. Ferguson, 163 U.S. 537 (1896); Civil Rights Cases, 109 U.S. 3 (1883); Dred Scott v. Sandford, 60 U.S. 393 (1856).

8. See Walker Lewis, *Without Fear or Favor* (Boston: Houghton Mifflin, 1965), 423.

9. *Dred Scott*, 60 U.S. at 404–5.

10. See Fredrickson, *The Arrogance of Race*, 189–205. Professor Fredrickson explores the relative tolerance in the 1600s and the transition to a "consistently racist society" beginning at the end of the seventeenth century. Judge Higginbotham documented this transition to a consistent and virulent racism in colonial America in A. L. Higginbotham, Jr., *In the Matter of Color: Race and the American Legal Process — The Colonial Period* (New York: Oxford University Press, 1978).

11. See Randall Kennedy, "Reconstruction and the Politics of Scholarship," *Yale Law Journal* 98 (1989): 521.

12. *Civil Rights Cases*, 109 U.S. 3 (1883).

13. Ibid. at 25.

14. Ibid. at 61 (Harlan, J., dissenting).

15. Ibid. at 17.

16. See Allen Weinstein and Frank Otto Gatell, *The Segregation Era, 1863–1954* (New York: Oxford University Press, 1970), 86.

17. *Civil Rights Cases*, 109 U.S. at 14.

18. Plessy v. Ferguson, 163 U.S. 537 (1896).

19. Ibid. at 550.

20. *Plessy*, 163 U.S. at 544. The formal equality of the statute was also expressed in the brief for the segregationist position: "[A]ny passenger insisting on going into a coach or compartment to which, by race, he does not belong, shall be liable to be punished according to its provisions. Should a *white* passenger [emphasis in original] insist on going into a coach or compartment to which by race he does not belong, he would thereby render himself liable to punishment according to this law. There is, therefore, no distinction or unjust discrimination in this respect on account of color." Brief of M. J. Cunningham, Attorney General of Louisiana, for Defendant in Error, at 14–15, Plessy v. Ferguson, 163 U.S. 537 (1896), reprinted in *Landmark Briefs and Arguments of the Supreme Court of the United States* 13 (Frederick, Md.: University Publications of America, 1975), 95–96.

21. *Plessy*, 163 U.S. at 551. The lawyers for Plessy tried unsuccessfully to return the argument to the plane of reality. "Perhaps it might not be inappropriate to suggest some questions which may aid in deciding this inquiry. How much would it be worth to a young man entering upon the practice of law, to be regarded as a white man rather than a colored one? Six-sevenths of the population are white. Nineteen-twentieths of the property of the country is owned by white people.

Ninety-nine hundredths of the business opportunities are in the control of white people. These propositions are rendered even more startling by the intensity of feeling which excludes the colored man from the friendship and companionship of the white man. Probably most white persons if given a choice, would prefer death to life in the United States as colored persons." Brief of James C. Walker, for Plaintiff in Error, at 9, Plessy v. Ferguson, 163 U.S. 537 (1896), reprinted in *Landmark Briefs* 13, 36.

22. "We imagine that the white race, at least, would not acquiesce in this assumption." *Plessy*, 163 U.S. at 551.

23. Ibid. at 552.

24. Brown v. Board of Education, 347 U.S. 483 (1954). See Richard Kluger, *Simple Justice: The History of Brown v. Board of Education and Black America's Struggle for Equality* (New York: Knopf, 1975).

25. Transcript of Oral Argument at 11, Davis v. Prince Edward County School Board, 347 U.S. 483 (1954) (argument of J. Lindsay Almond, Counsel for Appellees, County School Board of Prince Edward County, Virginia), reprinted in *Landmark Briefs* 49A, 512.

26. Transcript of Oral Argument at 69, Brown v. Board of Education, 347 U.S. 483 (1954) (argument of I. Beverly Lake on behalf of the State of North Carolina as Friend of the Court), reprinted in *Landmark Briefs* 49A, 1210, 1211.

27. Brief of John Ben Shepperd, Attorney General of Texas, Amicus Curiae at 3; Brown v. Board of Education, 347 U.S. 483 (1954), reprinted in *Landmark Briefs* 49A, 1042, 1044–55.

28. Ibid. at 5.

29. Ibid.

30. Transcript of Oral Argument at 13–14, Brown v. Board of Education, 347 U.S. 483 (1954) (argument of I. Beverly Lake on behalf of the State of North Carolina as Friend of the Court), reprinted in *Landmark Briefs* 49A, 1215, 1227–28.

31. Transcript of Oral Argument at 56, Brown v. Board of Education, 347 U.S. 483 (1954) (argument of John Ben Shepperd on behalf of the State of Texas as Friend of the Court), reprinted in *Landmark Briefs* 49A, 1265, 1270.

32. See W. H. Harbaugh, *Lawyer's Lawyer: The Life of John W. Davis* (New York: Oxford University Press, 1973).

33. Transcript of Oral Argument at 43, Brown v. Board of Education, 347 U.S. 483 (1954) (argument of John W. Davis on behalf of Appellees), reprinted in *Landmark Briefs* 49A, 465, 491.

34. Ibid. at 44, reprinted in *Landmark Briefs* 49A, 492.

35. Transcript of Oral Argument at 21, Brown v. Board of Education, 347 U.S. 483 (1954) (rebuttal argument of Thurgood Marshall on behalf of Appellants), reprinted in *Landmark Briefs* 49A, 515, 522 (1954–55).

36. *Brown*, 347 U.S. at 494.

37. Milliken v. Bradley, 418 U.S. 717 (1974).

38. City of Memphis v. Greene, 451 U.S. 100 (1981).

39. City of Richmond v. J. A. Croson Co., 488 U.S. 469 (1989).

40. *Milliken*, 418 U.S. at 746.

41. Ibid. at 739–41.

42. *Memphis*, 451 U.S. at 119–20.

43. Ibid. at 138 (Marshall, J., dissenting).

44. "But the evidence in this case, combined with a dab of common-sense, paints a far different picture from the one emerging from the majority's opinion." Ibid. at 155 (Marshall, J., dissenting).

45. Ibid. at 129.

46. Board of Regents v. Bakke, 438 U.S. 265 (1978).

47. Ibid. at 294 n. 34; ibid. at 298.

48. Ibid. at 309.

49. Ibid. at 400 (Marshall, J., dissenting).

50. In his treatise on the practical impossibility of emancipation, Professor Dew described the specter of black insurrection: "[H]is very worthlessness and degradation will stimulate him to deeds of rapine and vengeance; he will oftener engage in plots and massacres . . . every year you would hear of insurrections and plots, and every day would perhaps record a murder . . . the tender mother [would] shed the tear of horror over her babe as she clasped it to her bosom; others of a deeper dye would thicken upon us; those regions where the brightness of polished life has dawned and brightened into full day, would relapse into darkness, thick and full of horrors." Dew et al., *The Pro-Slavery Argument*, 444. Also see generally Kenneth M. Stampp, *The Peculiar Institution: Slavery in the Ante-Bellum South* (New York: Knopf, 1956).

51. *Richmond*, 488 U.S. at 552 (Marshall, J., dissenting).

52. "[T]he growing myth of the black man as a genetic sexual monster fanned the Negrophobia of the 1890s, a myth encouraged by novelists such as Thomas Nelson Page and later trumpeted by Thomas Dixon, Jr." James Kinney, *Amalgamation!* (Westport, Conn.: Greenwood Press, 1985), 153.

53. See Wyn Craig Wade, *The Fiery Cross: The Ku Klux Klan in America* (New York: Simon and Schuster, 1987), 119–39.

54. Charles Lawrence, "The Id, the Ego, and Equal Protection: Reckoning with Unconscious Racism," *Stanford Law Review* 39 (1987): 317. See also Joel Kovel, *White Racism: A Psychohistory* (New York: Pantheon Books, 1970).

55. See Lawrence, "Unconscious Racism," 322.

Chapter Three

1. Charles Burroughs, "A Discourse Delivered in the Chapel of the New Alms-House in Portsmouth, N.H.," quoted in Michael Katz, *The Undeserving Poor* (New York: Pantheon Books, 1989), 13.

2. See Joel Handler, "The Transformation of Aid to Families with Dependent Children: The Family Support Act in Historical Context," *New York University Review of Law and Social Change* 16 (1988): 479–80. "The foundation of the social welfare edifice erected by [Franklin Roosevelt's] administration became a distinction between public assistance and social insurance (relief based solely on need versus universal programs such as Social Security) that assured public policy would continue to discriminate invidiously among categories of dependent people." Katz, *The Undeserving Poor*, 15.

3. Ken Auletta, *The Underclass* (New York: Random House, 1982), xvi.

4. Katz, *The Undeserving Poor*, 277.

5. Ibid., 7.

6. See Robert Cover, "The Supreme Court, 1982 Term — Foreword: Nomos and Narrative," *Harvard Law Review* 97 (1983): 8. "Every denial of jurisdiction on the part of a court is an assertion of the power to determine jurisdiction and thus to constitute a norm."

7. Robert Cover, *Justice Accused* (New Haven: Yale University Press, 1975), 1.

8. Miller v. McQuerry, 17 F. Cas. 335, 339 (1853).

9. Cover, *Justice Accused*, 249.

10. City of New York vs. Miln, 36 U.S. 102 (1837). See Laurence Tribe, *American Constitutional Law* § 16–36, at 1627 (2d ed. 1988).

11. Ibid. at 142.

12. Goldberg v. Kelly, 397 U.S. 254, 265 (1970). See Charles A. Reich, "The New Property," *Yale Law Journal* 73 (1964): 733.

13. See Handler, "The Transformation of AFDC," 460. Earlier in this century, the program was overwhelmingly white as a result of the exclusion of poor black women: "In a 1931 survey, ninety-six percent of the participating families were white. . . . In North Carolina, there was only one black family enrolled. Hous-

ton, Texas, had none even though blacks constituted twenty-one percent of the city's population. In Marion County, Indiana (Indianapolis), where blacks comprised eleven percent of the population, there were no [black] families in the program." Ibid., 475 n. 76.

14. Dandridge v. Williams, 397 U.S. 471 (1970).

15. Ibid. at 486.

16. Ibid. at 484.

17. In the contemporary abortion debate, one of the few points of agreement shared by the advocates for each side is that the state has no business compelling abortions to limit family size. As a matter of constitutional law, the state is free, however, to create conditions that constrain the choice of the woman in poverty. The state may choose to fund childbirth but not abortion for the woman in poverty. See Maher v. Roe, 432 U.S. 464 (1977).

18. *Dandridge*, 397 U.S. at 487.

19. Wyman v. James, 400 U.S. 309 (1971).

20. Ibid. at 312, n. 4 (quoting N.Y. Code of Rules and Regulations, tit. 18, § 369.2).

21. Ibid. at 319.

22. Ibid. at 322 n. 9.

23. "[I]t is argued that the home visit is justified to protect dependent children from 'abuse' and 'exploitation.' These are heinous crimes, but they are not confined to indigent households. Would the majority sanction, in the absence of probable cause, compulsory visits to all American homes for the purpose of discovering child abuse? Or is this Court prepared to hold as a matter of constitutional law that a mother, merely because she is poor, is substantially more likely to injure or exploit her children? Such a categorical approach to an entire class of citizens would be dangerously at odds with the tenets of our democracy." Ibid. at 341–42 (Marshall, J., dissenting).

24. *Wyman*, 400 U.S. at 321–22.

25. Ibid. at 324.

26. Jefferson v. Hackney, 406 U.S. 535 (1972). The Texas state constitution originally prohibited all welfare payments. As of the time of the *Jefferson* case the state constitution limited state financing of welfare to $80,000,000. Ibid. at 537 n. 1.

27. Ibid. at 549.

28. Bowen v. Gilliard, 483 U.S. 587 (1987).

29. Ibid. at 610–11 (Brennan, J., dissenting).

30. Ibid. at 597–98.

31. Schweiker v. Chilicky, 487 U.S. 412 (1988).

32. Ibid. at 428–29.

33. Lyng v. Castillo, 477 U.S. 635, at 645 (Marshall, J., dissenting).

34. Richard Rorty, *Contingency, Irony, and Solidarity* (Cambridge, N.Y.: Cambridge University Press, 1989), xvi.

35. See James Agee and Walker Evans, *Let Us Now Praise Famous Men* (Boston: Houghton Mifflin, 1941); Mary Ellen Hombs and Mitch Snyder, *Homelessness in America: A Forced March to Nowhere* (Washington, D.C.: Community for Creative Non-Violence, 1986); Michael Katz, *In the Shadow of the Poorhouse: A Social History of Welfare in America* (New York: Basic Books, 1986); Jonathan Kozol, *Rachel and Her Children: Homeless Families in America* (New York: Crown Publishers, 1988).

36. *Dandridge*, 397 U.S. at 487.

37. Katz, *The Undeserving Poor*, 7.

38. See Cover, *Justice Accused*.

39. Max Black, *Models and Metaphors* (Ithaca, N.Y.: Cornell University Press, 1962), 41.

40. See my essay "Metaphor and Paradox," *Georgia Law Review* 23 (1989): 1053. Also see Cleanth Brooks, *The Well-Wrought Urn: Studies in the Structure of Poetry* (New York: Reynal and Hitchcock, 1947); Marcus Hester, *The Meaning of Poetic Metaphor: An Analysis in Light of Wittgenstein's Claim That Meaning Is Use* (The Hague; Paris: Mouton, 1967); Ricouer, "The Metaphorical Process as Cognition, Imagination, and Feeling," *Critical Inquiry* 5 (1978).

Chapter Four

1. Robert M. Cover, "The Supreme Court, 1982 Term — Foreward: Nomos and Narrative," *Harvard Law Review* 97 (1983): 4.

2. Any footnote listing of the examples will be incomplete. Among the important sources that have influenced my work are Catharine MacKinnon's books, *Feminism Unmodified* (Cambridge, Mass.: Harvard University Press, 1987) and *Toward a Feminist Theory of the State* (Cambridge, Mass.: Harvard University Press, 1989); Martha Minow, *Making All the Difference* (Ithaca, N.Y.: Cornell University Press, 1991); Patricia Williams, *The Alchemy of Race and Rights* (Cambridge, Mass.: Harvard University Press, 1991); Martha Fineman, "Dominant Discourse, Professional Language, and Legal Change in Child Custody Decisionmaking," *Harvard Law Review* 101 (1988); Lucinda Finley, "Breaking Women's Silence in the Law: The Dilemma of the Gendered Nature of Legal Reasoning," *Notre Dame Law Re-*

NOTES

view 64 (1989); Sylvia A. Law, "Rethinking Sex and the Constitution," *University of Pennsylvania Law Review* 132 (1984); Christine A. Littleton, "Reconstructing Sexual Equality," *California Law Review* 75 (1987); Martha Minow, "The Supreme Court, 1986 Term — Forward: Justice Engendered," *Harvard Law Review* 101 (1987); Robin West, "Jurisprudence and Gender," *University of Chicago Law Review* 55 (1988); Lucie E. White, "Subordination, Rhetorical Survival Skills, and Sunday Shoes: Notes on the Hearing of Mrs. G.," *Buffalo Law Review* 38 (1990); I also benefitted from reading Iris Marion Young's wonderful book *Justice and the Politics of Difference* (Princeton, N.J.: Princeton University Press, 1990).

3. See for example, Kimberle Crenshaw, "Demarginalizing the Intersection of Race and Sex: A Black Feminist Critique of Antidiscrimination Doctrine, Feminist Theory and Antiracist Politics," *University of Chicago Legal Forum*, 1989 (criticizing the tendency of legal scholarship to treat race and gender as mutually exclusive categories of experience and analysis); and Angela P. Harris, "Race and Essentialism in Feminist Legal Theory," *Stanford Law Review* 42 (1990) (discussing the work of Catharine MacKinnon and Robin West and arguing that, though powerful and brilliant, the work relies on gender essentialism with the result that some voices [those of black women] are silenced while others are privileged).

4. Katherine T. Bartlett, "Feminist Legal Methods," *Harvard Law Review* 103 (1990).

5. Ibid., 843.

6. Ibid., 831.

7. Ibid., 849.

8. Ibid., 864 (quoting Leslie Bender, "A Lawyer's Primer on Feminist Theory and Tort," *Journal of Legal Education* 38 [1988]: 9).

9. Cover, "Nomos and Narrative." Susan Koniak's article, "The Law Between the Bar and the State," *North Carolina Law Review* 70 (1992) provides an excellent synthesis of the heart of "Nomos and Narrative" and an exquisite application of those ideas to the legal profession. See also Drucilla Cornell, "From the Lighthouse: The Promise of Redemption and the Possibility of Legal Interpretation," *Cardozo Law Review* 11 (1990) (discussing Cover's work as part of her analysis of redemptive legal movements and the transformative effect of interpretation).

10. Cover, "Nomos and Narrative," 4–5.

11. Ibid., 5.

12. Ibid., 7.

13. Discussion of Bob Jones University v. United States, 461 U.S. 574 (1983) in Cover, "Nomos and Narrative," 62–67.

14. Ibid., 27 (quoting Brief Amicus Curiae in Support of Petition for Writ of Certiorari on Behalf of Church of God in Christ, Mennonite at 3–4, Bob Jones University [No. 81-3]).

15. Ibid.

16. Ibid., 9.

17. Ibid., 35–37.

18. Ibid., 38 (quoting Frederick Douglass, *Life and Times of Frederick Douglass*, R. Logan, ed. [New York: Collier Books, 1967], 261–62).

19. MacKinnon describes her vision of the brutal reality of the contemporary liberal state in the following terms: "The rule of law and the rule of men are one thing, indivisible, at once official and unofficial — officially circumscribed, unofficially not. State power, embodied in the law, exists throughout society as male power at the same time as the power of men over women throughout society is organized as the power of the state. . . . Male power is systemic. Coercive, legitimated, and epistemic, it *is* the regime." MacKinnon, *Toward a Feminist Theory of the State* (Cambridge, Mass.: Harvard University Press, 1989), 170.

20. See Catharine MacKinnon, *Sexual Harassment of Working Women: A Case of Sex Discrimination* (New Haven: Yale University Press, 1979); MacKinnon, *Toward a Feminist Theory*, 195–214 (discussing the constitutional protection of pornography as the legitimation of trafficking in women). MacKinnon's controversial promotion of an antipornography law is described in "Defining Law on the Feminist Frontier," *New York Times*, 6 October 1991, sec. 6, p. 29, col. 3.

21. Women committed to their vision of law can make a version of the move to insularity. They can create communes, for example, and construct their lives in ways that minimize the intervention of the state. But no such place will be wholly outside the influence of the state's law.

22. Susan Estrich, "Rape," *Yale Law Journal* 95 (1986): 1087.

23. Ibid.

24. State v. Alston, 312 S.E.2d 470 (N.C. 1984).

25. Estrich, "Rape," 1108.

26. Ibid., 1109.

27. State v. Lester, 321 S.E.2d 166 (N.C. Ct. App. 1984), *aff'd*, 330 S.E.2d 205 (N.C. 1985).

28. Estrich, "Rape," 1109–10.

29. *Lester*, 321 S.E.2d at 168 (emphasis in original).

30. Estrich, "Rape," 1111.

31. Ibid.

32. See Susan Estrich's book-length treatment of the subject, *Real Rape* (Cambridge, Mass.: Harvard University Press, 1987).

33. Estrich, "Rape," 1093.

34. See Carolyn Pesce, "Delicate Bra Is Permitted as Evidence," *USA Today*, 31 October 1991, 3A (reporting pretrial ruling by judge in William Kennedy Smith rape case); "Defendant Acquitted of Rape: 'She Asked For It,' Juror Says," *New York Times*, 7 October 1989, sec. 1, 6 (reporting statements of jurors in a Fort Lauderdale rape trial who acquitted defendant because they felt the woman "was up to no good the way she was dressed").

35. State v. Strickland, 351 S.E.2d 281 (N.C. 1987).

36. State v. Etheridge, 352 S.E.2d 673 (N.C. 1987).

37. See generally Susan Estrich, "Sex at Work," *Stanford Law Review* 43 (1991); Susan M. Mathews, "Title VII and Sexual Harassment: Beyond Damages Control," *Yale Journal of Law and Feminism* 3 (1991) (arguing that Title VII should be amended to allow recovery of compensatory and punitive damages and to incorporate appropriate evidentiary standards and burdens of proof).

38. Meritor Savings Bank v. Vinson, 477 U.S. 57 (1986).

39. Estrich, "Sex at Work."

40. *Vinson*, 477 U.S. at 68.

41. Estrich, "Sex at Work," 823.

42. Rabidue v. Osceola Refining Co., 805 F.2d 611 (6th Cir. 1986). See also Nancy Ehrenreich, "Pluralist Myths and Powerless Men: The Ideology of Reasonableness in Sexual Harassment Law," *Yale Law Journal* 99 (1990): 1193–1214 (analyzing the *Rabidue* opinion).

43. Estrich, "Sex at Work," 844.

44. Cover, "Nomos and Narrative," 39–40.

45. See generally Faye D. Ginsburg, *Contested Lives: The Abortion Debate in an American Community* (Berkeley, Calif.: University of California Press, 1989) (an account of the abortion conflict in Fargo, North Dakota, which contains "life stories" of women on both sides of the conflict); Susan Estrich and Kathleen Sullivan, "Abortion Politics: Writing for an Audience of One," *University of Pennsylvania Law Review* 138 (1989); Frances Olsen, "The Supreme Court, 1988 Term — Comment: Unraveling Compromise," *Harvard Law Review* 103 (1989).

46. See, e.g., Lynne N. Henderson, "Legality and Empathy," *Michigan Law Review* 85 (1987): 1635–37 (includes excerpts of women's letters collected by the National Abortion Rights Action League in its Brief as Amici Curiae in Support of Appellees, Thornburgh v. American College of Obstetricians and Gynecologists,

476 U.S. 747 [1986] [Nos. 84–495 & 84–1379]); Olsen, "Unraveling Compromise," (listing examples of situations in which women are forced or coerced into having sex).

47. The briefs filed on behalf of the State of Texas in Roe v. Wade, 410 U.S. 113 (1973), contained pictures of a fetus at various stages of development.

48. See, e.g., Stuart Elliot, "Anti-Abortion Campaign Causes Debate in the Industry," *New York Times*, 15 April 1992, D-20.

49. See Mary B. W. Tabor, "Life's Turns Lead to Abortion Barricades in Buffalo: Four Women and Two Men Talk of How the Issue Has Moved Them into the Streets," *New York Times*, 28 April 1992, B-1; Catherine S. Manegold, "Abortion War, Buffalo Front: Top Guns Use Battle Tactics," *New York Times*, 25 April 1992, 1.

50. Roe v. Wade, 410 U.S. 113 (1973).

51. 505 U.S. 833 (1992).

52. Ibid. at 846.

Chapter Five

1. Brief for Plaintiff in Error at 7–8, Plessy v. Ferguson, 163 U.S. 537 (1896), reprinted in *Landmark Briefs* 13, 10–11 (Brief of S. F. Phillips and F. D. McKenney).

2. Brief for Plaintiff in Error at 35–36, Plessy v. Ferguson, 163 U.S. 537 (1896), reprinted ibid. at 62–63 (Brief of James C. Walker and Albion Tourgee).

3. *Plessy*, 163 U.S. at 551.

4. Robert Cover, *Justice Accused* (New Haven: Yale University Press, 1975), 147–48.

Index

INDEX

INDEX

Library of Congress Cataloging-in-Publication Data
Ross, Thomas, 1949–
    Just stories : how the law embodies racism and bias /
Thomas Ross.
        p.   cm.
    Includes bibliographical references and index.
    ISBN 0-8070-4400-8
    1. Justice, Administration of—United States.
2. Judicial process—United States.   3. Bias
(Law)—United States.   I. Title.
KF384.R67   1996
347.73—dc20
[347.307]   95-48859